FRIENDSHIP & FAITH

the WISDOM of women
creating alliances for peace
By the Women of WISDOM

Women's Interfaith Solutions for Dialogue and Outreach in MetroDetroit

Friendship and Faith

The WISDOM of Women Creating Alliances for Peace

by the Women of WISDOM

Women's Interfaith Solutions for Dialogue and Outreach in MetroDetroit

Read The Spirit Books

an imprint of David Crumm Media, LLC

For ongoing discussion and additional material, visit
www.InterfaithWisdom.org

You may contact the author organization at
WISDOM@InterfaithWisdom.org

Cover art and design by
Rick Nease
www.RickNease.com

Published by Read the Spirit Books,
an imprint of David Crumm Media, LLC
42015 Ford Rd., Suite 234
Canton, Michigan 48187
U.S.A.

For information about customized editions, bulk purchases
or permissions, contact David Crumm Media, LLC at
info@DavidCrummMedia.com
734-751-7840
www.ReadTheSpirit.com

Contents

Author Acknowledgments   vi
Introduction   viii

Forming the Circle
WISDOM Co-Founders   2

Making Friends
Azar Alizadeh   18
Supreet Kaur Singh   24
Noelle Sutherland   28
Cheryl Zuhirah Ware El-Amin   32
Rehana Saleem Qureshi   38

Surprised by the Neighbors
Elaine Greenberg   44
The Rev. Sandra Kay Gordon   48
Mona Farroukh   54
Betty Sheehan   58
Gigi Salka   64
Padma Kuppa   70

Not Enemies After All
Motoko F. Huthwaite   78
Judy Goddard Satterthwaite   84
Shari Rogers   88
Sheri Schiff   94
The Rev. Sharon Buttry   100

Weaving Creative Ideas

Edith Broida   108
The Rev. Charlotte H. Sommers   112
Paula Drewek   116
Patty and Elana Haron   120
Brenda Naomi Rosenberg   126
Gail Katz   132

A Lifetime of Wider Vision

Elaine M. Schonberger   140
Ellen Ehrlich   144
Anjali Vale   148
Fran Shiovitz Hildebrandt   152
Shahina Begg   158
Sofia B. Latif   164

Author Acknowledgments

The main "authors" of this book are members of WISDOM: Women's Interfaith Solutions for Dialogue and Outreach in MetroDetroit. This network of women from many religious and cultural backgrounds now has years of experience in reaching out through public service, educational efforts and cross-cultural programs—sparking widespread interest in its unique approach to peacemaking.

In January of 2009, 14 WISDOM leaders gathered for a retreat at a Muslim center in Michigan, led by the Rev. Sharon Buttry, whose story appears in this collection. The retreat was called Building Bridges and, in it, the leaders explored ways to strengthen relationships between women and create innovative projects for the future. To deepen their reflections that weekend, the women divided into pairs—and one pair consisted of Gigi Salka, a Muslim woman, and Brenda Rosenberg, a Jewish peace activist. Their bridge-building conversations were so productive that Brenda proposed expanding this process far beyond the circle of WISDOM through a book of personal stories.

The group's enthusiastic response led to Brenda, Padma Kuppa, Sheri Schiff and Gail Katz, who is the current president of WISDOM, forming a task force to tell their own stories—and invite dozens of women from diverse backgrounds to contribute more stories.

As that creative circle expanded, WISDOM invited writers from a similarly wide range of backgrounds to help its members tell their stories. A year-long effort unfolded in which WISDOM women spent time with these writers who interviewed them, gathered background materials, and then helped them draft their final stories. The diversity in this creative effort crosses generations. Some of the writers are still in college—and some are veteran, nationally-known writers.

These co-authors include: Terry Ahwal, Kristina Birch, Amy Crumm, Debra B. Darvick, Stefanie DeHart, Stephanie Fenton, Sarah Fowlkes, Katie L. Miller, Patricia Montemurri and Frances Kai-Hwa Wang.

The WISDOM women told their stories to these writers in various forms, including taped oral histories, telephone interviews, written texts and, in some cases, archival documents and news clippings. After a co-author drafted a chapter, each woman further revised her story to make it fully her own narrative.

In this almost-exclusively women's production, three men also played key roles: Artist Rick Nease designed the book cover and Web graphics; Publisher John Hile designed the book's interior and aided in the project's research; and, finally, General Editor David Crumm coordinated the work of the 40 women contributing to the project—and edited the final collection of stories.

Introduction

This is a book about making and keeping friends.

That sounds so simple, yet there is a widespread need for help in navigating the complex friendships that often form today across a host of ethnic, religious and cultural divides. We spent a year talking with women from a range of cultural and professional backgrounds, asking a wide-open question: What could we offer in a book that would help women improve their own lives—and build stronger communities in the process? The answers could have ranged from interest in physical fitness principles to tips on organizing nonprofit groups.

The answer that came back in a virtually unanimous chorus was: Let's help women make friends.

The answers are different when we ask our wide-open question among men. Men tend to ask for instruction in spiritual disciplines, information on religious groups and tips for leadership. Men tend to want to prepare themselves to navigate the community successfully and, in the process, to make their mark on the world.

Women want to make a difference just as intently—but their first instinct is to work on forming the relationships that will knit the community together. They tend to reach toward one another, first, before reaching for their own individual toolboxes.

Those are sweeping conclusions that don't describe everyone. There are many men who think of relationships first in their spiritual journeys, and just as many women who want to start with professional training, educational principles and tips on best practices. There are women who are every bit as competitive as men in community relations. There are men who are every bit as nurturing as women in the relationships they hold.

Overall, though, we heard a loud and clear call from women: Give us a book about real people daring to cross boundaries to make friends. Tell us how they did it. Tell us why they needed a friend. Tell us about their anxieties as they reached out. Tell us some dramatic stories, but also tell us some ordinary, everyday, grassroots stories—about people just like us.

In 2008 and 2009, volumes 1 and 2 of *Interfaith Heroes* were published and circled the globe. These books now have been read by many men, women and youth, especially in the U.S., Europe and Asia. The first two volumes celebrate "famous people" who took risks to cross religious barriers. Not all of the heroes in these two volumes started from an auspicious background. Some did begin from positions of great privilege—but others attained their fame through their courage and grace under sometimes life-threatening circumstances.

In this collection, you'll find a few stories in which women faced substantial fears, for example: Motoko Huthwaite, now a noted educator and peace activist, tells about growing up as Japanese girl in America during World War II, when fear was rampant and friends were especially dear.

But in this collection, you'll also be welcomed into living rooms, classrooms, hospital rooms and offices where ordinary people interact and make choices that you can make, as well.

As we wrote in both volume 1 and volume 2 of this series, the purpose of celebrating interfaith heroes is to inspire more people—and, as you read these pages, to inspire you, personally, to become the next hero to step forward.

As you'll learn in this, volume 3, there's probably someone right next to you for whom a friend would make all the difference in the world.

—*David Crumm, General Editor*

(David Crumm is the founding editor of ReadTheSpirit.com, an online magazine, and of Read The Spirit Books. David is a journalist with more than 30 years of experience who served as General Editor for this book, coordinating the year-long project that produced this final collection of stories.)

PART I

Forming
the Circle

CHAPTER 1

WISDOM Co-Founders
Forming the Circle

Men generally begin by trying to resolve the issue—often without initially building the relationships that make resolution more probable.

Gail Katz is Jewish, Shahina Begg is Muslim and Patricia "Trish" Harris is Catholic. Gail and Shahina contributed individual stories found in this book. All three met and became friends through connections with an innovative interfaith project called "Reuniting the Children of Abraham," developed by Brenda Rosenberg, whose story also appears in this volume.

As we open this collection of stories about friendship and faith, Gail, Shahina and Trish talk about how their friendships evolved and expanded into an organization: WISDOM (Women's Interfaith Solutions for Dialogue and Outreach in MetroDetroit.) As you enjoy their story, look for echoes of other stories you'll read in this book. In the end, the creative work of an organization like WISDOM is possible only through a wide network of relationships.

G AIL: This story begins at a time when each of us had our own reasons why we were attracted to forming a women's interfaith group but, even though each of us had had those reasons for a number of years, we hadn't really been acting on them. In fact, we might never have even met had it not been for "Reuniting the Children of Abraham."

I got involved with "Reuniting the Children of Abraham" back when it was in the form of a play, performed in various places. As an educator, I had been involved in diversity programs for young people for years. I had seen the play quite early on at the Jewish Ensemble Theater in the West Bloomfield Jewish Community Center, and I was just blown away by it, which is why I agreed to be a facilitator for students. After these performances, I worked with groups of middle-school students, talking about what they had just experienced.

TRISH: The play is part of my story, too. I'd saved the playbill from my first experience viewing "Reuniting the Children of Abraham" in 2004, because I was so powerfully moved by it. You know, it's entirely possible that, over the years, the three of us may have attended some of the same events, but we never met until 2006.

SHAHINA: I do recall seeing Gail much earlier, at an interfaith event where she was leading a group of students, but I didn't formally meet her then.

My own interfaith journey, like so many of the women in WISDOM, goes back a very long way. In my life, it goes back to my childhood in India and to marrying my husband, Victor, who is Muslim. I had grown up Hindu and converted to Islam in 1975. Victor and I always were interested in interfaith work. When Brenda Rosenberg created "Reuniting the Children of Abraham," our daughter, Sofia, agreed to help Brenda in writing parts of what became the final production.

So I always felt very close to that production and attended presentations whenever I could.

Later, there was a documentary created about the "Reuniting the Children of Abraham" process. Brenda invited me to come and see the documentary when it was shown for the first time at Kirk in the Hills Presbyterian Church in Bloomfield Hills, Michigan. This was the spring of 2006 and I excitedly accepted the invitation. I have always been interested in visiting various places of worship, and as I had often driven past this beautiful church, I was especially looking forward to this event.

GAIL: We all had been involved in some way with diversity initiatives, but we did not get to know one another before that event at Kirk in the Hills. In fact, I didn't actually meet Trish that night, but our connections began there.

TRISH: I was there that night at the Kirk. I had read about the premiere in my church's bulletin and, remembering the production from almost two years before, I was eager to see the documentary. I had been so impressed by the production that I actually bought eight extra tickets so some of my friends could attend the documentary showing. That night at the Kirk was an important time because it brought together hundreds of people who were interested in this kind of work—many for the first time.

GAIL: I did meet Shahina that night. I had already met her husband, Victor, at various interfaith events, but I had never had a chance to meet his wife. That evening I also met Peggy Kalis, who would become a co-founder of WISDOM, but who has since moved out of the Metro Detroit area. At that time, Peggy Kalis was a member of a local Unity church and was very active in interfaith work.

SHAHINA: There was a "talk back" opportunity after "Reuniting the Children of Abraham" was shown that night.

I was so inspired after seeing the documentary and hearing the responses from the participants in that debriefing session.

During the reception that followed the event, I had a conversation with Barbara Clevenger, who is a Unity minister. I said, "Wouldn't it be nice for women of many faith traditions to work together in the same way that the teens in 'Reuniting the Children of Abraham' collaborated together in the making of their production, but with an emphasis on things like community service projects?"

Barbara said, "Let me introduce you to someone who would be very interested in this idea." She introduced me to Peggy Kalis and, right away, something clicked. I remember that Peggy talked to me about a visit she had made to an open house at a mosque in Canton, Michigan. She had taken part in some prayers there and had had a very positive experience. She said that she wanted to work on more opportunities like this for women, and I knew immediately that we had a lot in common.

GAIL: At the end of the Kirk program, there was a social time for chatting and eating. My husband and I began talking with other Jewish folks we knew, and we might have visited only with those friends that night. But, the next thing I knew, this complete stranger—Peggy Kalis—came right up to me. I think someone had pointed me out to her in the crowd, because of my educational work in diversity.

Peggy said, "Perhaps you might be interested in putting together an initiative to get women together to talk about their faith traditions, like the young adults have done in 'Reuniting the Children of Abraham.'"

My first reaction was: No way! I'm already running the Religious Diversity Journeys for seventh-graders in Oakland County. I'm already the chair of the annual World Sabbath service, an interfaith event that focuses on youth. I was doing so much already. How could I take on another committee?

That's what I thought this was—just another committee forming.

I didn't say it that way to Peggy, though. I listened to her politely. I felt tense as she began to talk about this. After a while—and maybe she sensed what I was feeling—she finally said, "How about if we just meet for coffee?"

I agreed to that with some reservations, thinking that this was as far as I'd let this relationship go.

Then, I talked with Shahina that evening as well, and I began to think: You know, this really is right up my alley—women reaching out to other women who might not get to meet one another because of close-knit circles of friends and family members within their own faith traditions.

TRISH: The documentary premiere was only the start of this effort toward interfaith dialogue. Meanwhile, four local places of worship had committed to hosting a day during the following month for people who wanted to experience their worship service, ask questions and enjoy refreshments and fellowship afterwards. Kirk in the Hills Presbyterian, the Muslim Unity Center, Temple Beth El and St. Hugo of the Hills Catholic Church all participated. I had wanted to attend all four programs, but was out of town for the weekends that the mosque and the temple held their programs. I was able to attend the ones at the Kirk and St. Hugo's. It was at St. Hugo's that I met Shahina.

SHAHINA: That was a wonderful event! After the Mass, there was a question-and-answer session. That was the first time I had been at a Catholic church, and it provided me an opportunity to clarify some of the questions I had. Interfaith gatherings like these begin to break down our stereotypes and misunderstandings so that our conversations can begin to flow openly.

TRISH: After the Q&A session, we all walked down to the parish hall to enjoy a buffet and some further discussion. I was one of the first to arrive, and I'd decided to sit at an empty table, hoping that people I didn't know might join me. An imam, Victor, and Shahina sat down at my table, and I spent the rest of the afternoon talking with Shahina.

SHAHINA: We had such a nice conversation that day. We started out talking about our backgrounds and then ventured on to other topics. I don't think Trish had met many Muslims before that point, had you?

TRISH: No, up to this time I had only had casual professional acquaintances with Muslims at work, but I hadn't really interacted with Muslims socially or discussed their faith with them.

SHAHINA: At St. Hugo's that day, I remember we talked for quite a while. It was very casual and comfortable. This was the same way I had felt when I met Gail for the first time. We hit it off immediately.

TRISH: I told Shahina: "I'm sorry that I missed the program at the Muslim Unity Center."

She said, "Don't feel bad! We're having an Open House. Come to our Open House!"

SHAHINA: That's right! I invited you to the mosque that day.

TRISH: But before the date of that Open House at the Muslim Unity Center, there was one more service in the series, at Kirk in the Hills. I attended that event and, once again, I ended up connecting with Shahina. She repeated her invitation to come to the Open House at her mosque. This additional meeting was important, because as the date for the Open House drew nearer, I had begun to get cold feet. I wanted to go, but was a little afraid of going alone into an unknown environment. My curiosity and the rapport that had built up between Shahina and me gave me the "push" I needed to attend. Getting to know this one person opened the door for me to expand my worldview.

SHAHINA: We had spent so much time planning for that special day at the Unity Center! We wanted to teach people about the history of Islam, but we also wanted them to feel welcome and to simply get to know us. Our hope was to live up to the Unity Center's founding values of unity and diversity, by bringing people of varying ethnic and cultural backgrounds together.

TRISH: That Open House was so much fun. I thought I'd be there for maybe 40 minutes, but ended up staying for three hours. Once again, I saw Shahina right away, and she began introducing me to more people. I ended up doing everything the hosts had planned. I toured the mosque, saw a video on Islam, had my picture taken in a "desert" tent, collected pamphlets on Islam and ate wonderful Middle Eastern food.

As I was getting ready to leave the mosque, I saw Shahina and sat down for a moment to thank her for a wonderful afternoon. During the course of my goodbye, I shared something with her that had been on my mind for some time. This was sparked by my experience with the original production and by my participation in "Reuniting the Children of Abraham" over the last month—a desire to do something together as "Women of Abraham."

I remember Shahina looking at me and saying, "Funny you should mention that. Two other women are interested in doing something like that as well. Would you like to join us for coffee?"

GAIL: What Trish didn't know is that this was the coffee date that we had planned way back at the Kirk. I knew that I was planning to have coffee with Peggy and Shahina, but then this fourth woman showed up, whom I didn't know at all: Trish.

That coffee date turned out to be the key moment when all four of the WISDOM co-founders were together for the first time!

TRISH: It's likely that we had been in the same crowd together somewhere previously, but this was the first time that we had knowingly been together—all four of us around the table for conversation.

GAIL: From the start, we didn't do much with the "Women of Abraham" phrase, because we didn't want to limit the group to women from the Abrahamic faiths: Judaism, Christianity and Islam. We wanted to be open to Hindus, Jains and others, too.

TRISH: That was an eye-opener for me. What I had experienced so far was the "Reuniting the Children of Abraham" approach, including only the "People of the Book": Jews, Christians and Muslims. The other women had a much broader vision. Our scope came to include any and all women, regardless of faith tradition, and included those of no faith tradition. As we talked more, it became clear to me that I was the "novice" in interfaith matters. Gail had "lived" interfaith for much of her life, and was sincerely devoted to repairing the world. Shahina had an international background and had been instrumental in the founding of a mosque that brought Muslims of different ethnic and national backgrounds together. Peggy worked for a Christian faith-based organization and had many ties to various charities. I was a little overwhelmed by my lack of experience, knowledge and networking in interfaith work.

SHAHINA: That first meeting was important, but it wasn't an ideal setting. There were a lot of people there in that coffee shop—a lot of noise. It wasn't a good place to talk too much about our lives.

GAIL: I could see that, too, and finally I said, "You know what? Let's make a dinner date at my house where we really can talk. We can spend hours, if we want."

Our coffee meeting was in May of 2006 and that same month the four of us met at my home for dinner. We set no agenda that night. I suppose that if men are talking about an idea for a new organization, they may start with an agenda before they do anything else. But what women do is sit down around a table and start talking.

That's what we did. We didn't have any formal plan. We began sharing and soon, we were speaking from the heart with one another.

SHAHINA: Everyone was so open and candid. We delved straight into some deep questions. "What's your story?" "Where do you come from?" "What's your history?"

GAIL: "What are your interests?""Tell us about your children.""Do you have a significant other?""What challenges do you have in your life now?""Where have you traveled?""Where have you worked?""What's really important to you in your faith tradition?" We connected on all kinds of levels. We talked and talked—and talked—that night.

We did conclude with: "What should we do now?" But nearly all of the evening was spent sharing our personal stories honestly with one another.

SHAHINA: There was no leader in that circle. We each told our stories as equals.

GAIL: We must have spent at least three or four hours with one another. We weren't thinking of the time. It just flew by.

SHAHINA: At that point, we weren't even thinking about the specific details of the project itself. That wasn't as important as getting to know one another, first.

GAIL: The four of us must have met four or five times before we ever got down to talking about specific details of a program. Finally, we agreed that we all wanted to bring more women together. For that, we needed an event—an opportunity for more women to form relationships, like we were doing. Our first meetings together were in the spring of 2006 and we planned our first large event for that August.

That's when we turned to a detailed planning process. That's also when we began to realize how important this work was. That was the summer of the Israel-Hezbollah War. My husband and I went on a vacation at the end of July, and I took my laptop along and checked in on my interfaith work. Soon, I was reading emails firing back and forth between Jews and Muslims over the war, and it was very heated. Some of the exchanges were downright ugly. I was beginning to pull my hair out with concern and total frustration.

I remember one prominent religious leader saying: "I am no longer going to be involved in interfaith programs"—and he left a group in which he'd played an important role. He just pulled out, because he felt that he could not interact with the local Muslims. I was horrified.

We already had our first WISDOM program on the docket. When I got home from the vacation, I thought: Look what's going on in the world! Look what's happening with relationships in our own community! I was so distraught.

Our first large event was on August 20, 2006. We had invited women to work together on a local Habitat for Humanity building site. We had no idea what to expect.

TRISH: This was our first event. I was excited and scared. Would people actually show up? Would they work together? Would our opening ceremony touch people and not turn them off? Would our icebreakers work during the lunch break? Would the participants have enough time to get to know one another? Would they feel that they had done something meaningful for themselves and for the community?

SHAHINA: That day, we were scheduled to work on installing windows and siding on two homes. Most of the women who had signed up had no experience with construction, so we were all a little nervous about who would show up.

GAIL: From this first event—and continuing with every other interfaith initiative that we've put together in WISDOM—we've committed ourselves to very careful planning. We work hard on this. People have to register. We make sure people will be comfortable. We ensure that people will interact with folks of different faith traditions.

Still, we all were blown away at the Habitat site when 55 women actually showed up. With everything else going on in the world, with some skepticism from other people about what we were doing—they came!

TRISH: We started that day in a park near the homes where we would be working. We formed a big circle of women and we had several different people offer prayers from their different faith traditions. Those opening prayers set the intention for the entire day. After we explained how the day would unfold, the Habitat for Humanity staff briefed us on the different jobs that we could perform throughout the day.

GAIL: We had planned the whole day. Big sheets were laid out on the grass for the women to sit on during the lunch break. We structured the break so that all the Christians didn't wind up in one corner and all the Muslims in another corner.

We provided them with icebreaker questions. We usually do that in our events, because it's too easy to fall into talking about something like—you know, what's on TV that week. So, we provide questions to help get the conversations going in a meaningful direction. We might ask: "How did you get your name?""What does your name mean?""What's your most prized possession?""What's a family tradition within your religion that you participate in each year?"

That day at the Habitat site, with all of those women sitting down to lunch—we could tell it was working when the volume of conversation began to rise everywhere. We actually had women telling us they wanted more time to talk, and were reluctant to break off the conversations to go back to work.

TRISH: But the women were also very committed to the work we had gathered to accomplish that day. When we had to call a halt to the construction, clean up the site and put away the tools, everyone was so involved with this joint initiative that no one wanted to stop. The evaluations indicated that the women were proud of what they were able to accomplish, and the only negative comment related to wanting more time to do more work on the houses together.

GAIL: At the end of the day, we came back together and formed our big circle again. We sang a Beatles song.

TRISH: We sang *Give Peace a Chance.*

GAIL: I know this is a Beatles song—and that may sound odd. It isn't a traditional faith-based song. But I couldn't help but to get all choked up in that circle, singing that song, and I know I wasn't the only one who felt that way. We were so connected that day. We had done something that was useful. We had helped two families who needed these homes. We had come together as women from many different faiths and we had gotten to know one another through the whole experience. We connected at a deep, spiritual level.

TRISH: There had been a lot of pre-event apprehension. But as the day progressed, there was a palpable feeling of confidence that arose among us. The all-women crew—most of whom had little or no construction experience—was able, with direction from the Habitat staff, to contribute significantly to the construction projects. The women's overwhelmingly positive approval of the event, their desire to be included in future events and the friendships made that day showed us that we could organize a successful interfaith event—and our confidence grew.

GAIL: That's a central part of everything we do together—empowering women to do new things!

I've been involved in interfaith work for years, but WISDOM has changed my life. I've grown a great deal in at least two areas. One of the areas in which I've grown involves organizational skills, and much of what I've learned is from working with my buddy, Trish. Through this work together, I've helped to organize all kinds of educational events and community service projects. I am the president of WISDOM and have a board of directors consisting of women of eight different religions, which includes an executive board, and I've learned a lot about what really works when you're trying to bring people together to make a difference in your community.

The other major change in my life is my deep desire to learn more about my own Jewish tradition. I have been very committed to furthering my Jewish education, and it has become very clear to me that I have a burning desire to connect with my own Judaism on a very spiritual level. In getting to know this diverse group of women, I've deepened my own faith.

TRISH: The same thing has happened to me. Skills I used in my professional career have been directly applicable to the founding and development of WISDOM, and the programs we have coordinated. I have also developed some new skills that would never have come about otherwise. My WISDOM interactions and friendships have challenged me to re-examine my own faith in an effort to explain it to others. My faith and worldview have been both deepened and expanded.

SHAHINA: I've experienced the same thing. I realized that I didn't know as much as I should know about Islam. Anytime people would ask me questions, I was hesitant to answer because I wasn't sure I was giving an accurate answer. I've signed up for classes, too, to learn more about Islam, and I really look forward to them.

My friendship with Gail, Trish, Peggy and others has deepened the spirituality in so many aspects of my life. I realize that amidst all of the planning and coordinating and organizational work that we do, what I really value most is the bond that we have built. I truly cherish the knowledge that no matter what is going on in the world, that I have these friends upon whom I can rely.

TRISH: In the end, everything we've done through WISDOM begins with faith and with the relationships we have been able to build together.

There is something distinctive, generally speaking, about how women work together. We tend to take the time to build the relationships first, and then work on solving the problem. When we add faith to those relationships, we find that it gives us the strength needed to deepen our understanding of, our respect for and our connections with one another. Men generally begin by trying to resolve the issue—often without initially building the relationships that make resolution more probable.

GAIL: Our goal is not to solve the Middle East problem or to get involved with worldwide political differences. We are trying to break down barriers, to increase respect and understanding, and to dispel myths and stereotypes here, locally, in our communities. We have learned that we can change lives, strengthen our communities and be a model for others, if we don't lose sight of the fact that this process begins by forming relationships—one friend at a time!

PART II

Making
Friends

CHAPTER 2

Azar Alizadeh

A Friendship Despite a Secret

"This just doesn't make sense!"
I said. It seemed so unfair.

Azar was born in Iran and is a fourth-generation Baha'i. She has been a U.S. citizen since 1975 and, in recent years, has hosted a weekly public television program in Michigan called *Interfaith Odyssey.*

When I was growing up, my best friend kept a secret from me for a long time.

Let me tell you that story ...

I grew up on the north side of Tehran, Iran, in a happy family. My father had a store that sold imported fabrics from Europe. Our house was made up of two flats; we lived downstairs, and my aunt lived upstairs. My grandparents lived about a mile away from us.

Most of the people in Iran are Muslim, but I grew up around people of other faiths as well. There were some Jewish people, some Zoroastrians and I am a fourth-generation Baha'i. In the 1950s—under the Shah, things were not easy for Baha'is—conditions were not as bad as they became later. We heard the Shah had a doctor who was Baha'i.

We felt secure, even though sometimes bad things happened. In my third-grade class in the public school, I was singled out by a teacher who asked Baha'i students to raise their hands. I know three of us in that class were Baha'i, but I wasn't as smart as the others. I actually raised my hand. The teacher singled me out to go sit in the corner, and she punished me by saying that I had to hold one of my feet off the floor for a while. All of this only because I was Baha'i.

Later, my parents moved me to a private school. My best friend through these years was named Tahmineh, a Muslim girl whose family lived near mine in Tehran. She had a very good sense of humor, and I did, too. We became best friends and we often walked back and forth to school together, or sometimes took a bus.

Tahmineh and I were selected by the producer of a national radio show who was looking for children to appear in weekly broadcasts from Tehran—so that was something else I shared with Tahmineh. This was a children's program that aired every Friday, which is like Sunday in the U.S. It was an idea similar to *Sesame Street*. These were not religious broadcasts, but just nice weekly stories for children with good lessons behind them. Every week there was a different story about 20 or 25 minutes long. The children who worked with the show each played a part in telling the story. The director and producer would meet with us to show us our parts so we could practice. It was a lot of fun. I had a great-aunt who lived far away from us, but she would say, "Every Friday, I can turn on the radio and know that you are doing well, because I hear your voice on the radio!"

Tahmineh and I spent a lot of time together. There was no way, just by looking at us, that one could tell that Tahmineh was Muslim and I was Baha'i. We wore the same kinds of clothes. During the Shah's regime, women did not cover their hair as much.

We visited each other's homes. At first, we played together. As we got older, we read books together or listened to the radio. We'd spend an hour or two together visiting like this in our homes. Eventually I began to notice that, when I visited Tahmineh's house, her mother would give us things to eat, but I could not recall Tahmineh eating anything at my house.

One day, when we were about 12 or 13, I visited her house and her mother gave me something good to eat. This time, I said, "Tahmineh never eats at our house."

There was silence. They didn't say anything. I knew that there was something they did not want to talk about, so I let the subject drop.

The next day when Tahmineh and I were walking to school, I asked, "Why is it that you never eat our food? Don't you like our food? When I asked about this yesterday at your house, no one answered me."

Again, there was silence. We had never talked about this before. Finally, she said, "It's a secret."

"A secret?" I said, "Tell me! Tell me!"

Then she explained, "My parents say that Baha'is put things in their food and drink that will make other people become Baha'i."

I didn't cry, but this hurt me; we were just children, and this was painful. I told her: "Tahmineh! This is just a myth!"

The secret was out and, as we talked, we both understood what had happened. There was a fanatical mullah (an Islamic clergyman) who was spreading hatred against Baha'is across the country. One of the myths that he was spreading was this claim that Baha'is had things they would mix into food and drink to convert people. Tahmineh's parents had heard this and had refused to let her eat at our house.

She said to me, "I've always known it's a myth. I know that, but I didn't know what to do! My parents told me never to eat at your house. But, I love you. I love your parents. I don't want to hurt you."

"This just doesn't make sense!" I said. It seemed so unfair. I thought: Oh, her parents are so mean! Then, I said to my friend, "Tahmineh, you must not eat at our house. I won't offer you food at my home anymore. You've got to do what your parents say." That was a very important thing we were taught in Baha'i Sunday School—always follow what your parents tell you. There was no question about disobeying her parents.

We were best friends—now closer than ever. I hoped we would get around this somehow, and we did. I told my parents about it, but I never said a word to her parents. I kept Tahmineh's secret with her family.

Then, do you know what we did? We started going to the neighborhood store together, because there we could buy things and eat them together on neutral ground. We enjoyed candies. We loved ice cream. Now, that was fun!

That was a difficult experience for a girl. Tahmineh and I were friends. We loved each other, yet she had heard this terrible thing about my family from her parents and she carried that secret for a long time. Through the years, I have lost track of her; in 1960, my family moved to Germany and later I moved to the United States and became a citizen. I'd love to find my friend again. I've Googled her and I keep looking for her on Facebook, but her name probably has changed through marriage.

I am hopeful about the future. We all are born to do something for the betterment of humanity. We need to share our stories, like this one, to help encourage a greater understanding of our diversity. The world's many different faiths are all gifts from God for us. If we just set our individual egos aside a little bit, we can see that truth.

Children understand it. I have seen the goodness in children myself. It melts my heart when I see friendships made—and kept—between different faiths. Sometimes that may mean sharing each other's secrets, but it is through friendship that we can see hope for our world.

CHAPTER 3

Supreet Kaur Singh
Often, We Stand Alone

A lot of people I come across in daily life think I'm a Hindu. I tell them I'm a Sikh, and they say, "Okay." That doesn't mean anything to them.

The stories in this book are about friendship and Supreet, as a lifelong Sikh, has found important friendships through the interfaith women's group WISDOM. In Supreet's story, she conveys the uncomfortable feeling of isolation that many people feel when they are part of smaller religious groups. This is especially poignant for Sikhs because their sacred traditions require them to dress in ways that make them visual targets whenever they travel in America.

I grew up in India, and at that time, I had friends who were Hindu, Christian and Muslim. I was brought up around people of different backgrounds and different religions.

But in India, Sikhs are a minority. And, often, minorities aren't considered as important as the majority. People would make jokes about Sikhs—would make fun of us—and we couldn't do much or say much because we were the minority.

Later, we lived through a few years when attacks were made on Sikhs. In 1984, Indira Gandhi, the Prime Minister of India, was attacked and murdered by some people who were Sikhs. After that, there was turbulence throughout India and a lot of innocent Sikhs were killed. The Sikhs were not prepared for these brutal attacks. Many died. *The Widow Colony: India's Unsettled Settlement* is a 2006 documentary film that shows what happened in 1984 and afterward.

We Sikhs need to tell the story of our faith more widely. Most people have heard the word "Sikh" and know that it is the name of a person of our faith, but they don't know more than that. Most people don't know the significance of men wearing a turban (a turban is supposed to give the look of a saint, or of a holy person). They don't know that we believe in eating *jhatka* meat, meat from an animal that was killed in our traditional way with no pain.

The word "*jhatka*" is like the word Jewish people use for properly prepared food: kosher. Or Muslims say: halal. Everyone has an idea what it means when he or she hears someone use the word "kosher." But, when I am at a restaurant, it is hard to find someone to ask about whether any of the meat is *jhatka*. No one even knows the word, in most cases. Our process of preparing the meat follows principles similar to kosher or halal preparation—but our traditions are different and the process is different. Imagine the difficulty we face at restaurants, if we want to eat meat. Of course, some Sikhs don't eat meat at all.

Living in a minority community is difficult enough, but the media add to the problem by portraying Sikhs on TV and in movies in stereotypical roles. Sikh men and women have few opportunities in the entertainment business, so it becomes easier for people who write and produce TV shows and movies to feel they can make fun of Sikhs.

I have lived with this difficult challenge all my life. Now, when my sons go to a mall, they get noticed, too. We do try to explain who we are, if people ask, but many people don't really want to learn much.

A lot of people I come across in daily life think I'm a Hindu. I tell them I'm a Sikh, and they say, "Okay." That doesn't mean anything to them.

Now, I do have some American friends who are not Sikhs. We Sikhs believe in hospitality and welcoming people who are not a part of our faith. We welcome people to visit our *gurdwaras*, our houses of worship. Anyone can go, not just Sikhs. The WISDOM women understand this. In WISDOM, we welcome everyone of every faith, too. We talk about the meaning of our beliefs and traditions.

I am hopeful that people will want to learn more and will want to make friends from other faiths—if we give them opportunities like this. In my own life, I find that if someone is willing to tell me about their religion, I think it is amazing.

I think others will find all of the world's different faiths amazing, too.

CHAPTER 4

Noelle Sutherland
New Friends and Old Friends

> *I'm human. I get afraid. I don't want to ruin things with friends.*

Noelle grew up in a household with little interest in religion, but she became curious as a teenager and sampled a wide range of religious experiences. When she got married in 2002 and started her own family, she and her husband decided to make religious practice a central part of their home. They joined a little-known religious group within Buddhism. In the previous chapter, Supreet Kaur Singh describes the challenges of growing up within a religious minority. But what happens when, as an adult, you become a part of a small religious group? What happens with old friends when your life changes and you meet new friends?

I have some friends who have been extremely accepting about our religion. They've seen how much it has changed my life in positive ways. They've asked questions about it, and I'm happy to answer their questions. But mostly these are friends I've met more recently—friends who haven't known me for years. There are old friends who I still haven't told that I'm now Buddhist.

My husband and I follow Nichiren Daishonin Buddhism, and most of the followers worldwide are Japanese. I'm not. I'm Caucasian. I grew up in the Midwest. My family has lived in Michigan forever. So, this is quite different for people who knew me years ago while I was growing up. I have a master's degree and I'm a middle-school teacher of science and social studies. I hadn't really found a religion for myself, but my husband and I—as we met and eventually got married—discovered that we both had this strong connection with Buddhism and the various philosophies and practices within Buddhism. We had both been reading about it, we discovered! My husband had a whole collection of books about Buddhism. While I hadn't had any religious upbringing, he came from a family that was very strongly Roman Catholic. So, this was new and quite different for both of us—but we both felt this very strong connection to Buddhism.

We had not really acted on that, but when we were married I got pregnant right away. We both realized: We've got a family coming—we should go ahead and find someplace to attend. We began trying different churches, and one day we met some people who were practicing Nichiren Buddhism. Very quickly we found that—my gosh—everything about their practice was exactly what we were looking for.

We became Nichiren Buddhist about six years ago. Nichiren Daishonin was a Japanese monk born in Japan in 1222. Basically, we follow the *Lotus Sutra*, writings of Nichiren

Diashonin, and chant *Nam-myoho-renge-kyo* daily. Buddhism is a mainstream religion, and Nichiren Buddhism is growing in size, but there aren't a lot of people who practice this in Michigan.

We practice in our homes, where we also hold meetings. We also attend monthly meetings at a community center. We have potlucks. You might think that my son, growing up in the suburbs, would be getting a steady diet of pizza and hamburgers. But, because most of the people in Nichiren Buddhism are from Asia, my son is growing up eating curry and sushi regularly.

This choice we've made has been absolutely wonderful for my husband and our family, but it has been a struggle for me in other ways. We live in a mostly Christian society in this country, and I guess a lot of people don't realize how important the Asian influence has become. Millions of Americans are practicing yoga, and Asian religious traditions are a growing part of this country's culture—but some people are not very accepting of our choice.

I've had people look at me and say: "You're an American Caucasian woman—so how can you be a Buddhist?"

Even though we've spent years with our religious practice, I still haven't worked out how to relate to all of my old friends. There are still some who knew me years ago who I haven't talked with about this. I'm not sure what their reactions would be.

This has been a very good choice for us. People who know me can see that I've got a lot more optimism about life now, but there is a fear in some friendships. I'm human. I get afraid. I don't want to ruin things with friends. I do wonder: Will I be judged by a different standard if this person knows my religious experiences are not the same as most people?

It's a lot easier for me to form new friendships. When I make new friends, things aren't so difficult. I just describe who I am. This is all just a part of my life. New friends get to know the person I am today. Buddhism is a large part of my life, and I don't find that I need to explain myself, only explain what they might not know about my religion.

What I fear is that someone I knew in the past won't respect the importance of my choices. I don't want to hear them saying, "Oh, this is just a phase you're going through." And, I don't want to hear them say, "Oh, it's just a bandwagon she's jumping on."

In some ways, I wish I had been born into Buddhism. There's a phrase, "fortune babies"—for people who were born and grew up in the religion. When you're born into it, you've got all the confidence and all the knowledge of your tradition from so many years of living within it.

But there are a lot of Americans like me, who look around for the religion that's right for them—and who do make changes. Millions of Americans are making new religious choices. I hope that more people will become accepting of these choices.

I know it's possible. At a wedding, I found myself sitting at a table with a girlfriend from college. She's a Christian but she is very open to new ideas. We got to talking about what we believe. I told her about my practice—and she was interested in my story. We had a good and very lengthy discussion. She made me feel confident in the way she responded. It was a wonderful experience.

I wish people would stay open-minded, like this friend I met again at the wedding. The key is acceptance. I don't like the word "tolerate." As a teacher, I can "tolerate" kids at school, but that's not enough for strong relationships between friends. We need more than that in our relationships. Acceptance truly helps to make our lives better.

CHAPTER 5

Cheryl Zuhirah Ware El-Amin

"Working Hard" with Co-workers

It's so easy to misunderstand other people if you don't have an opportunity to talk honestly.

Cheryl was raised Presbyterian, then converted to Islam in 1976. Her lifelong pursuit of education led her to obtain a doctorate in 2009 in human services with a specialty in clinical social work. She is a school social worker and also is active in charitable and religious groups, including the mosque where her husband is the assistant imam.

I am a quiet person. I grew up as an only child, without a lot of other children running around our home, but I have always enjoyed meeting new people—especially people from other faiths and ethnic backgrounds. After my years of training in social work, I've learned not to be judgmental of others. When I meet people, I try to relate to them just as they are. I always assume that people have an essence of good within them, and I always try to relate to someone's best essence.

I have a longtime friend whom I met back in the late 1980s; I remember that she was the first Caucasian person with whom I developed a close friendship. We were both social workers at a hospital. When I was hired, I was assigned to share an office with her—and it was not a big office, so we got to know each other right away.

We shared several things: We both had a Presbyterian background; we both had grown up as an only child; and we both now had children of our own. We talked honestly as colleagues—and, as we got to know each other, we also talked just as girlfriends. We would joke sometimes as we found ourselves discussing people's assumptions about race and ethnicity.

We encountered some of those stereotypes we discussed right there at the hospital. She is about 10 years older than me, and I'm African-American. We shared a small office space. So, occasionally, when she was out of the office, I'd find people sticking their head in our doorway and giving me messages for her. It was obvious that they took one look at me and just assumed I was her secretary.

I didn't get angry at such things, but I did correct people. I'd say: "I am not her secretary. But I will tell her when I see her."

There are a lot of assumptions people carry around with them that are difficult to get rid of, because people often feel awkward talking about them. I remember one woman calling me on the telephone because she wanted to clear up a few things in her head about this "black thing."

I remember she asked me, "Are you enraged?" She said, "I've heard that because of all the years of oppression in African-American history, there's this underlying anger." I guess she thought we all automatically shared this kind of free-floating anger and that we were all enraged. She called me with this question because she was concerned about a relationship with another African-American person. She thought she would double-check her assumptions about this "black thing" with someone who might explain it to her honestly.

I explained that there's a lot of diversity among people. I do feel strongly about many things, but the idea that we all carry around the same free-floating feelings? Well, speaking for myself, I've never felt the kind of rage she described. I have been militant about some issues over the years that have mattered to me, but I don't carry a permanent rage. The real point here is that people are diverse.

I also discovered that I, myself, had assumptions about race. As my work continued at the hospital and I became better friends with this woman in the office, I began to realize that I had been making some assumptions about white people. I realized that there were far more Caucasian ethnicities and backgrounds than I had realized before. I had tended to mentally lump white people into one group without many distinctions, and my friend was happy to talk about this, especially when we'd encounter some new person. She might say: Oh, well, *this* person comes from a particular ethnic background and there are a lot of distinctive cultural issues here. Or, we might talk about social distinctions. She might say: Now, *that* person is what we'd call "old money," and people from that background tend to have *these* kinds of experiences.

I enjoyed our conversations. It's so easy to misunderstand other people if you don't have an opportunity to talk honestly.

We were good friends for a while, and then we went through years when we didn't see each other. I took a job in school social work and she moved to a different hospital. We kept in touch occasionally by email until one day, about a year ago, when she remembered that my husband enjoys golf and picked up the telephone to tell me about a golf tournament near her home. She had tickets to the tournament and thought my husband might enjoy seeing it. I stopped by her new hospital to pick up the tickets and, after that, our friendship picked up again.

Some time after that, my husband and I renewed our wedding vows after 31 years of marriage and she came to that. It was wonderful. She got to see my children again, all grown up now.

As a Muslim woman, I know how many misperceptions there are about us. People assume that, since I cover my hair now, I'm forced to do that. And that's just not true. It's a choice I've made. I didn't always cover my hair; I choose to do that now. No one is forcing me.

Here's another example: People will say, "Oh, you're Muslim, so you don't believe in Jesus."

And I say, "What? That's not true. I believe in Jesus. I don't believe he was God, but Jesus is a very important part of Islam."

I've come to see that working on relationships with other people is a lifelong process. It really is. There's a verse in the Quran from Surah 94 that reads:

When thou art free (from thine immediate task), still labour hard, And to thy Lord turn (all) thy attention.

What it means is: You're never really finished with anything. When you're free from your immediate task, keep working hard, because there's still more to be done. The passage says "with every difficulty, there is relief." So, there is encouragement along the way, but we're not supposed to fall into contentment and inactivity. In our relationships, especially, we need to keep working. You never really "arrive" in life. You're always arriving—G'd willing.

CHAPTER 6

Rehana Saleem Qureshi

Reaching Out and Reaching Within

If we had stayed inside our Muslim box, we would have grown anxious, afraid. Instead, we held Open Houses. We invited people to come inside.

Now 60 with a grown daughter of her own, Rehana reflects on a lifetime of navigating friendships both within the close bonds of the Muslim community and in the larger world of diverse cultures. Education is one key in forming such healthy relationships, she says.

We moved from India to Pakistan when I was little. We had to make this difficult move with nothing—just the clothes on our backs. When we moved, we were four sisters, then three more sisters were born in Pakistan—so we were seven sisters in all. Through these years, we became a very close family.

Education is so important in life. My parents raised us in a home with Shakespeare and *National Geographic Magazine*. We read about new things in publications my father ordered from England. I remember my sisters and I would sit down together and read articles about how to do new things, like knitting, sewing and cooking new foods.

Eventually, my family decided to move to the U.S. and, over a period of about 10 years, relatives helped one another to migrate. I came in 1973. I got married and moved to Fort Wayne, Indiana. I studied to become a medical technologist and, for 22 years, I worked at the Detroit Medical Center in the microbiology department.

I am a moderate person. I'm very open to friends of different faiths and cultures. I worked in the medical community, so I have Christian, Jewish and Hindu friends and I know that we are all the same as people. We all have families and we all face problems in life—often in very much the same ways, whatever faith we may be.

As parents, my husband and I put a high value on education and carefully selected schools for our daughter. When our daughter was young, we chose a day care center called Kinderkirk, where she got along very well with children from other cultural and religious backgrounds.

As I was growing up, I attended Catholic schools through my college years. It was a good education and I found the nuns to be very dedicated. They helped to mold my character into the woman that I am today. But I was growing up in a

Muslim community, in a Muslim country. My daughter was growing up in a country where most people are not Muslim. It is important to learn about your own faith.

So, my husband and I—together with many friends—began to work on establishing a Muslim center in Canton, a town west of Detroit, where we live. In the beginning, we would rent a hall when we got together or sometimes we met in someone's basement. Twenty-five or 30 families would gather for potlucks. We organized ourselves and worked on establishing our own place. The women helped to raise the money to build our school and community hall. This was difficult, but we knew that we were laying the foundation of our faith for our children, so we worked hard. One year we raised $80,000 by catering for all kinds of occasions like weddings and other events.

The families that helped were Muslim, but they also were diverse—from many different places. Some were Pakistani and Indian, some were Egyptian, others were Libyan. They were from many places.

My daughter studied for a number of years in a Muslim school, and she was a good student. Then, after eighth grade, we moved her to a Catholic school. She's quite athletic and, at her new school, she joined the track team and the ski team. Today, she continues those passions by running marathons and designing soccer shoes for a living. I am glad that she had this mix in her schooling. The Islamic schools helped her to hold onto values that come from our religion—like not drinking. With friends now, she often is the designated driver, because people know that she doesn't drink.

Some people have this idea that Islam is such a strict religion that its members can't even talk with people of other faiths; and that might be the case for some Muslims, but I am very broad-minded, and I feel that people must interact with one another outside of their own little boxes.

If we don't do this, it is easy to become afraid.

When my Muslim community began building up the Muslim center in Canton, there was some community opposition around us from non-Muslims who wondered what this place was going to become. If we had stayed inside our Muslim box, we would have grown anxious, afraid. Instead, we held Open Houses. We invited people to come inside. We welcomed so many people that I remember going into a drug store one day and being surprised to find that a woman working behind the counter knew me already! The woman had come to one of our Open Houses and had enjoyed it so much that she greeted me in the store.

I know that not everyone is as open as I am, but I do think that this is the way to make the world a safer place for all of us. We need education. We need relationships with people from different countries and cultures. Once we make friends with people, they aren't just Muslims or Hindus or Christians—they become our friends.

Life is short. I'm 60 now. I look in the mirror and say: Oh, my! It's like I blinked my eyes and suddenly I am now this old. But even at my age, there is still work to do. God wants to strengthen us all in this way—through drawing us closer to one another. There is too much violence in the world today because of the ignorance between people. Every time I pick up a newspaper, I wonder: Where is all of this taking us?

In recent years, I joined this new group of educated women, WISDOM, so that I could learn more about other religious traditions. For example: Baha'is. I didn't know much about Baha'is before I joined WISDOM. And do you know what happened to me? This new group made me go deeper into my own religion! Now, I am always wanting to learn more so that I can talk intelligently to other people about Islam.

I know there are other women like me. Perhaps if more of us pursue learning and friendships that cross our many traditions, we actually *can* make a difference where we are living. And after that? Perhaps we can reach out beyond our own cubbyhole and make a difference across the country. And someday? We might be able to make a difference in the wider world.

Part III

Surprised by
the Neighbors

CHAPTER 7

Elaine Greenberg
Holidays and Huffy Neighbors

*You can imagine the alterca-
tion that followed! It ended
with our neighbor walking
out of our house in a huff,
mumbling something about
"Jews."*

Elaine Greenberg is a musi-
cian, a cancer survivor and
an active member of her
Jewish community. For
many years, she led choirs
and taught music—and now
she uses her own vocal talents to help cancer patients
and their caregivers.

When I was a young girl, Hanukkah was not a big holiday, and gift-giving was not what it is today, so our family—my uncles, aunts, grandmother—put our names in a container, and everyone picked out one name and that was the person they were to buy a gift for. My Uncle Hy had my name one year and bought the complete score (on 78 records) of Walt Disney's *Snow White and The Seven Dwarfs*. I still have that album. When my children were small, my family still wasn't making a big deal about Hanukah, but one year we decided to give the children eight gifts—one for each night of the holiday. I tried to be very clever, and on the last night, each one of our children—ages 4 to 10 (well, maybe not the 4-year-old)—got a key to the house. They thought that was fabulous! How times have changed!

But my favorite story of all is from the earlier years of my life.

This goes all the way back to 1944, when I was just about to turn 9 years old and my mother and father finally saved enough money to buy us our very own home. Such excitement! The house was everything my parents could have asked for, with the exception of the outer color of the house, which was dark red, almost brown, and the ceiling in the kitchen, which was a blinding, bright red.

We had a fireplace, although it wasn't lit too terribly often. To my father's delight, we even had a screened-in porch that ran the entire width of the house. My father spent many a hot summer night sleeping on that porch and, since there was no such thing as air conditioning, we all spent many summer days and nights on that front porch.

In the corner of the kitchen, there was a small shelf about chest-high that served as a telephone shelf. On the white walls surrounding that telephone shelf were a ton of telephone numbers. You see, my father would call Information (no charge in those days) and didn't have paper readily available, so he wrote the numbers on the kitchen walls. I do believe, when we sold that house, the numbers were still on the walls.

On one side of this house, we had what was called a four-flat where four separate families lived. But on the other side of our house, there was a single-family dwelling that was somewhat smaller than ours. The husband and wife who lived there were Frank and Marie Honel.

Unfortunately, our first encounter with the Honels was not a pleasant one. It involved a lamp that had come with our new home—one of those things the previous owners had left behind.

When Mrs. Honel paid us her very first visit, we found out that she and her husband had come from Germany in 1938. When we moved into our home in 1944, the war was still going on in Europe, so here we had a Jewish family and a German family living next door to each other. In itself, this could have caused problems.

But the lamp touched off the conflict. Mrs. Honel came to visit us because she insisted that the previous owners were aware of her affection for this particular lamp—and had promised that it would be given to her in the transition. When the lamp never made it to Mrs. Honel's house, she apparently decided she would come over and claim it from the home's new occupants. My mother knew nothing about this supposed arrangement. In fact, she rather liked that lamp.

You can imagine the altercation that followed! It ended with our neighbor walking out of our house in a huff, mumbling something about "Jews." We didn't speak to them for quite a while. I don't know how long.

But, eventually, a kind of peace settled in between the two families.

When our neighbors emigrated from Germany, they brought with them a household full of furniture. Their house was cozy and comfortable with antiques and all kinds of other interesting stuff they brought with them from their homeland.

Among their belongings were beautiful Christmas decorations, including heirloom tree ornaments that they used every year.

Mr. and Mrs. Honel had no children. As I recall it, Mrs. Honel seemed almost reluctant one winter when she surprised me by asking if I would like to trim their Christmas tree with them. Their ornaments were beautiful, and I wanted to help.

I had to ask for my parents' permission, of course. They were Orthodox Jews, but my mother still gave her permission. And we hit it off! From then on, the Honel tree wasn't trimmed until "their girl"—and that was me—was there to help them.

How well I remember those figures under their tree that depicted the birth of Jesus.

Of course, I didn't know that one day I would visit Israel and, as part of my trip, I would visit Bethlehem and see where Jesus was born.

We even exchanged gifts. The Honels got Christmas gifts from us. We got Hanukah gifts from them.

I treasure those memories of sitting in their home, a young girl sharing with this elderly couple. In their wonderful kitchen, I would talk with Mrs. Honel as I helped her bake goodies in an old-fashioned wood-burning stove.

Why do I cherish this memory?

Because of the love I felt in that connection with the Honels—and the forgiveness that allowed us finally to cross over all that had separated us and finally share that love.

CHAPTER 8

The Rev. Sandra Kay Gordon

A Surprise in a Hospital Room

Driving home—if I tell this story honestly—I didn't think I'd ever see her again.

The Rev. Sandra Gordon has been an active Baptist all her life and felt a calling to ordained ministry in the 1990s. Before that, she had worked in a bank, for a government agency and as a day care provider. Throughout her life, she's had a passion for bridging gaps between cultural communities—and lives a legacy of her parents' approach to life and faith.

I can see now that I've been on a long journey of making connections between Judaism and Christianity, but it took an encounter with a young Jewish woman in a hospital room to turn up some of the stereotypes I had accumulated while growing up.

My family is Baptist, although we had known Jewish people through the years; my family had Jewish doctors while I was growing up, for example. But I really did not know much about Judaism when my first daughter was born in 1974. I had never had a Jewish friend.

That's why I was surprised on the day my daughter was born. From recovery, the hospital staff moved me to the room I would share during my stay at the hospital. The first thing I could see from the doorway was that I barely had a space in there! This other family had packed that room with flowers, balloons and lots of people. The other mother's name was Sarah, and the nurses actually had to ask her family to clear some space for me.

They were Jewish, and everybody in her whole extended family was making a big hoopla over her child.

Their affection and generosity and joy toward this baby were all very impressive to me, but I have to admit—my reaction also reopened stereotypes I'd heard from my peers while growing up. The assumptions people passed around when I was growing up were old stereotypes—you know—like the one that Jews have a lot of money; that Caucasians, in general, didn't like us; and that Caucasians lived out in the suburbs because they didn't want relationships with us. I could see that this family cared a whole lot about Sarah and her baby. But just one look at all the stuff in that room—all the gifts and flowers—told me these people had money.

As a little girl, I had experienced racism firsthand. In 1959, my family traveled back to my father's hometown in South

Carolina for a family funeral. I was absolutely shocked when I saw doors labeled for "Whites" and other doors labeled for us. Then, my cousins invited me to go to the movies, and I was horrified to find that we couldn't just walk up to the front doors—only white people could do that. We were just children, but we were forced to walk around into the alley where there was a door back there, labeled for us to use. I realize now how much that experience traumatized me. I do remember that I cried all the way home from South Carolina. How could the world be so hateful?

I did have one big advantage growing up, because in my home, these biases were never taught against any group of people. My father worked for Chevrolet and my mother's jobs included working for the Catholic Archdiocese of Detroit; my parents never taught negative things about Jewish or Caucasian people. They worked with people from other cultures. So, I had my parents' balance in my life as well.

Now, I have to admit that on that day, when I walked into the hospital room with Sarah and her family filling the whole place—yes, I was a little jealous of Sarah.

I was a first-time mother, too. She had this whole garden sprouting over on her side of the room; I had one little, bitty flower someone had given me. With all of the gifts she had over there, on her side of the room, it was obvious they were rich. I got a few things, but nothing like that pile over on her side.

Now—truth be told—her baby was the very first grandchild on both sides of the family, so it was a very special event. In my family, mine wasn't the first grandchild—so, that was one big difference.

These events all took place back in the day, when mothers stayed in the hospital for a while and, as I recall, both Sarah and I had longer stays because of some complications. So we knew we'd be living side-by-side in that room for a while.

There was a curtain between the two beds, but we decided not to pull it—and, I'm so glad we didn't close that curtain! Instead, we began to talk. When all the visitors left, we were just two young mothers, talking about our lives and families and hopes for the future. We were tired, of course, but we sat up talking until the wee hours of the morning. She was so down-to-Earth, so pleasant, so kind. She became a good friend that first night.

But, I will tell you, there came a time when she left—a day or two before I did—and you know how, after something like that, people always say, "Oh, we'll be sure to get together!" Well, we did—and she actually did invite me to her house.

I debated whether to go. Did she really want me to come? Would I be comfortable? Would I know all the right things to do in her home? But I am an extroverted person, and I went out there, even though I was nervous. It turned out to be just great! She served lunch, and we put our babies down on the floor together. We talked and talked. When it was over, I said what you would expect: "Now, you'll have to come to my house."

Driving home—if I tell this story honestly—I didn't think I'd ever see her again. It was one thing for me to drive out to her house, but she had to come into Detroit to visit mine. It was one thing for us to visit just once, like we'd promised when she left the hospital. But to continue this as a real friendship? No, I didn't think it would happen.

Again, she surprised me. She really did want to come to my house. She had no problem coming into Detroit. She visited, and I served *her* lunch this time. Our babies played on the floor together and, once again, we talked and talked.

That friendship continued for a couple of years. I've lost track of her now, as sometimes happens with friends as years go by—but she was an important friend in my life.

What about all those old biases I had learned from my peers while growing up? They faded away. Now, looking back, I realize that I've always been on a pathway connecting my Christianity with the traditions of our Jewish neighbors. Now, I'm the assistant to the pastor at a nationally-known church in Detroit: Greater New Mount Moriah, which once was pastored by the Rev. Benjamin L. Hooks, Ph.D., head of the NAACP. He retired some years ago and I work with our senior pastor—the Rev. Kenneth J. Flowers, who also is well-known for his work linking Christians and Jews. In 2008, I visited Israel and learned even more about how our faiths and histories connect in so many ways.

I'd like Sarah to know that our friendship was an important part of my own journey, from all that I saw in childhood—some of it quite traumatic—to the calling that I have today to spread the word about all the ways that Christians and Jews, together, can strengthen each other's lives.

CHAPTER 9

Mona Farroukh
The Tiny Mighty

To live in the land of the free is one thing, but to actually live the life of the free is another.

Mona, Muslim from birth, found an all-too-common barrier preventing her from reaching out more widely in her community: an abusive spouse. Ending her marriage finally freed her to imagine how much larger her network of relationships could be. She now is a leader in her community, speaking about her experiences to help other women.

I love this country. I can come and go as I please, laugh when I want, and do what I enjoy. But there was a day, even though I lived here in the United States, when embracing these freedoms was impossible. I am so glad that day is behind me.

I grew up knowing I wanted to make my mother proud. She raised my sister and me on her own—a single mother in Beirut, Lebanon, raising her daughters in the midst of a civil war. My heart ached to honor her, to justify the sacrifices she made for my sister and me. But not until I'd been married for 16 years did I realize that I would have to divorce my husband in order to live the life I envisioned for myself.

Abuse is a widespread captor. For years, I endured because I thought it was best to keep the family together. Finally, however, I decided that keeping my family together was not protecting anyone, but instead was hurting us all.

Divorcing my husband was taboo in my Muslim community, as was speaking out about abuse. In ending my marriage, I also shed my *hijab*, a traditional head covering for many Muslim women. Removing that veil, a symbol which, to me, represented the voiceless and painful darkness in which I had lived for 16 years, was like lifting the curtain to my soul. The woman that had been locked inside for so long was finally set free.

My newfound freedom was not without conflict, though.

My mother taught me that people are good and are the same beneath their apparent differences. She taught me that I could accomplish anything, and she made my sister and me attend school, which was not required for girls in Lebanon. My mother also taught me that I am worthy—that my life has meaning. For a while, these beliefs lay dormant in my life. Finally, they could blossom and make me the woman I am today.

I returned to school, completing my bachelor's degree. This was wonderful. Many teachers inspired me, and one in particular helped me to see the world from new perspectives. I began to understand more about my role in the world.

After graduating with my bachelor's, I began working. My desire now is to help improve the health and well-being of the men, women and children of the Arab-American community. I strive to empower others, to plant in them the beliefs that my mother implanted in me. I am blessed to be able to do this work.

In 2007 I was awarded the Spirit Award by the Wayne County Prosecutor's Office. People in my community call me the "Tiny Mighty"—tiny, in that I stand less than five feet tall, and mighty, in that I am driven to give a voice to the voiceless. I have also been called "Phoenix," one who rose from the ashes with determination to live and to provide a decent life for her children. I've been called "The Lotus Flower," a symbol of rebirth. Such acknowledgement only encourages me to aim higher. I am now back in school, obtaining my master's and hoping to study for my Ph.D. My dream is to become an inspirational public speaker on empowering communities, especially for women.

To live in the land of the free is one thing, but to actually live the life of the free is another.

I no longer dream of honoring my mother. It now is a part of my everyday life—all I have to do is choose, each day, to make her proud.

Now, I know that can be done.

CHAPTER 10

Betty Sheehan
All the Same in Our Souls

My mother opened the door—and I will never forget her face! She looked stunned. Why wouldn't she talk to Favor? This was my best friend.

Betty Sheehan is a Catholic director of religious education. She also has worked with incarcerated teens. Her strong belief in justice and peace led her to become an active member in interfaith groups. She and her husband, Bob, have nine children and seven grandchildren.

"We want you back! We want you back!" I heard my mother say.

I was 5 years old and unconscious from a fever so high my family thought I had died. With my sense of hearing taken over with my mother's cries, I had a vision. (I never told anyone in my family but my grandmother. Why? I don't know. You always share with your grandma.) But there in the grip of that fever I had a vision—of the Blessed Virgin Mother. There she was before me—her palms were open to me and I reached out to take her hands. But as I reached for her, she raised her palms.

"No," She said. "You can't come yet. It's too soon."

From that moment, I felt that vision was a call to me. Calling me to do God's work in whatever way I can. In my Catholic faith I'm known as one who is kind of different. Maybe it's because I felt I was called. Maybe it's because of the way I approach life. Maybe it's because I never had to overcome accepting people of other races or cultures. We are all the same within our souls. I've never felt any other way.

I am the director of the religious education program at my church, and it is my belief that religious education works when the students feel positive reinforcement through praise and acknowledgment—and there are parents, guardians or grandparents who set a primary example for their children by their own faith actions. We have volunteers who willingly give of their time to share in the ministry of "echoing the Word of God." There's not an age of a child I do not love!

Because these children are our progeny, I realize that passing on religious traditions requires the whole community. It is my prayer that when setting up programs, I never forget the importance of inclusion, because we are all the same within our souls and justice and peace will only occur if it begins with us.

I've gone to two WISDOM Sister Circles and what amazed me both times was how all of us came together—we had Hindu women, Muslim, Baha'i, a Roman Catholic like me, a Jewish woman. The topic of one evening was anger. I sat back and listened to all the conversations, and I'm telling you, everything they said was common to us all. We all have hurts; we all have angers. We're all seeking love and forgiveness, and the way we choose to seek love and forgiveness—the way we express it—is what makes us different. But if you sit back and listen, we're all saying the same things. The Abrahamic story is for everyone. I realized there is no difference in faith; our souls all have the same struggles. At least, that's how I've always approached life.

Nothing I do is on my own; I don't feel I am an entity unto myself. Each day I pray, "God, let me do Your work this day." When I speak to teens and children, I pray, "God, let my words be Your words. Let Your words work through me." I work with teens who have attempted suicide. I think the number one cause for these attempts is that these children believe that no one is there for them—someone who knows they are special. If they can just believe there is one God, Allah, the Most High, they won't give up.

Same with the elderly. I think a lot of times the elderly are simply misdiagnosed. What is diagnosed as depression is the feeling that they are no longer valued. They are lost—a forgotten generation. We don't realize the beauty and history that they can share. That's why I invite my grandmothers to come in and help in ways they feel comfortable (reading, listening to prayers, baking). That's why I bring my teens in to help the younger classes. Every person has value. Every person has something to give.

So here's what I do with my Confirmation students: I pair them up with an elderly person in the parish, someone 70 or 80 years old. They do not meet at first, but are simply given each other's names and are told to pray for each other. Come

Thanksgiving, I have the teens make a meal for their prayer friend. That's when they meet for the first time. And when they are confirmed, their senior buddy packs them a lunch and writes them a letter.

Like I said, every person on this Earth has value. Every person has something to give.

When my husband's work transferred us to Mexico, the generosity I witnessed stayed with me long after we moved to Detroit. In Mexico, people were poor as heck but they opened their homes to us. They shared what they had. It was culture shock for my kids, let me tell you. My 6-year-old couldn't understand it. Seeing 4-year-olds begging was shocking! One day, my daughter saw a barefoot child and tried to take off her own shoes to give them to the child. I think those years in Mexico are the reason all four of my children are very much givers. You can't come back from there and say, "I have nothing," when we are so blessed. I have lights in my home I can turn on. I know my house will be warm in the winter. I have clean water to drink.

I think that you are somewhere for a reason, there is a reason why things happen.

I have been out to the New Mexico desert and have visited the tribe called the "Corn Huskers," and to Canada to visit the Chippewas. What may appear as different is truly the same. The Native American tribe danced with corn—dressed only in corn husks–and passed out loaves of cornbread. Yet, what was so apparent was the common thread of "sharing and breaking bread among others."

The Eucharistic bread, in my Catholic faith, is considered the source and summit of coming to the table. The Canadian tribe celebrated with the "Prayer to the Four Winds," a prayer which gives thanks, adoration and praise to the Creator for the circle of life and its blessings. It, too, parallels the Catholic faith's acknowledgment of God's grace through the Sacraments, which celebrates the life given to us by God.

Ceremonies may certainly differ, but if we are going to come together in this world, we have to have acceptance before understanding. If we can't open our doors in our personal communities to people who are different because of their color or creed, how can we expect nations to do so?

Here's a story about opening doors. It happened to me in first grade:

My best friend's name was Favor. I told my mother all about her, how we ate lunch together every day, and—could I please bring her home with me? What I didn't tell her, because I hadn't realized it, was that Favor was black.

The day came, and Favor and I walked home from school. My mother opened the door—and I will never forget her face! She looked stunned. Why wouldn't she talk to Favor? This was my best friend.

We played the whole afternoon, and after she left, my mother said, "You can't bring her back anymore. If she comes again, people will talk." I knew right away there was something wrong with that.

Only years later did I learn, from my aunt, that four African-American girls had once jumped my mother on a bus and tried to rob her. That's when I realized she had been afraid for me all those years ago. My mother was a warm and giving person, always reaching out to people. Her reaction to Favor was so out of character. All I knew that afternoon was she didn't like my friend.

You have to be open with children. If my mother had been open with me, she might have been able to see Favor as I did: she was my friend. I would have had the opportunity to talk about it, and talking at least opens the door to conversation. But to be open, you first must recognize your fears and then ask yourself if your fears are justified or are only misconceptions. Maybe my mother would have understood what life has taught me—we are all the same in our souls.

CHAPTER 11

Gigi Salka
The Hardest Thing I've Ever Had to Do

I was nervous. Anxious. Worried. All of the above! People don't know how to react when you make a change like this.

Gigi is Muslim and the mother of three children living in Bloomfield Hills. She is an active volunteer in her community.

The hardest thing I've ever had to do in my life was to walk into my child's school for the first time after I began wearing the headscarf that is distinctive for Muslim women. My son was in fifth grade at the time.

This all happened in February 2003. My husband and I finally decided to perform the pilgrimage, the Hajj. We had wanted to make the Hajj for years but, each time, something would come up. There always seemed to be so many reasons why we shouldn't go. The kids were too young. My husband couldn't leave work. It was a very serious decision. As Muslims we like to say that, when you go on the Hajj, you come back home the way you were born. It's like all your sins are erased and you're opening a new book in your life. For me, I knew that meant I would start wearing the headscarf.

I had not been wearing the headscarf and, because I hadn't worn it, I didn't stick out so obviously as Muslim in public. Just look at me and my kids—white, blond hair—we kind of blend into the American environment. But the question of wearing the headscarf had been weighing on my shoulders for some time. I grew up in America, attended university, had a successful career, married a loving husband and began raising my family. God has blessed me with so much. I wanted to start wearing the headscarf regularly as a sign of my faith, but I didn't have the strength.

It wasn't a big struggle for me to decide whether I should wear it. I wanted to wear it. I had already begun to change how I dressed. I only wore long skirts or pants and long-sleeve shirts. It is all about being modest; in dress, in attitude and in self-presentation. In my opinion, the headscarf was just another step toward greater modesty, but I could not garner the strength to put it on and wear it regularly. The biggest problem for me was the idea of facing people I had known for a long time—now wearing the headscarf. That's hard for many American Muslim women, I think. I know it was for me.

When we went on the Hajj, though, I knew that I'd definitely want to start covering my hair.

As the Hajj season nears each year, the excitement in the Muslim community grows. People start talking about who is going on the Hajj this year, and how they are preparing for this once-in-a-lifetime trip. Every year I remained at home, yearning to join the pilgrims, but this year was different: There were so many friends planning their trip that it was impossible to stay away. Although, in retrospect, it was probably the most inopportune time, my husband and I decided at the last minute to perform the Hajj that year. We were so late in deciding that we wound up Federal Expressing our passports, and we didn't get our travel documents until we got to the airport. We were hurrying around and weren't even sure that we'd be able to make the flight, but finally, we did get on the plane. This was a rushed trip, but I felt a sense of inner peace and security that I had never felt before. God gave me patience.

As we were hurrying around and getting ready to go, a Muslim friend came to visit and say goodbye. When I saw her, I suddenly had all these questions. I asked, "When am I going to put my headscarf on? The imam is coming with us on the plane, so should I put it on before I get on the plane? Should I put it on over there in Saudi Arabia? Or, when I'm coming home? How do I wear it right?"

So many questions!

She said: "Just put it on! Get it over with!"

So, I put it on as we went to the airport. Women wear the headscarf throughout the entire Hajj in Saudi Arabia. Then, when we were coming home on the plane, once again there were all these questions! I kept asking my husband: "Do I keep it on? Do I wear it when I get off the plane? What am I going to do?"

He was of no help. "It is your decision," was the answer he repeated over and over again.

I got home and basically stayed at home for a week. I kept worrying: What do I do? I can't take it off and, if I go out wearing it, what will people think when they see me for the first time?

Then, soon, I had to face going into my children's school. I'm very active there. I couldn't stay away. There was a parent meeting I had to attend. Coming back from the Hajj, I did feel spiritually rejuvenated and stronger as a Muslim, but on that first day walking toward the school, I couldn't stop asking myself: How will people react?

I hadn't planned anything that I might say to people. If they asked questions, I would try to answer them. That's how I am. But I really didn't know what I would say to explain it all as I drove up that day. Our school is designed so there's a parking lot and then there's a *loooong* sidewalk that leads up to the school. There's no way around it. You have to park and walk up this *loooong* sidewalk.

I parked my minivan and I made that walk very *sloooowly*.

No one at the school knew I had gone on Hajj or that I would start wearing this scarf. And on that first day that I went to the school, I knew that my son's teacher had gone on maternity leave while we were away, so I didn't know the new teacher at all. I was nervous.

Anxious.

Worried.

All of the above!

People don't know how to react when you make a change like this, so it puts more of a burden on you to break the ice. They wonder: Am I supposed to say something? Or not say something? Respond to this change? Or ask something? Or is it offensive to ask questions?

Finally, I reached the door. I walked into the school and, as soon as you walk in there's this media center where people congregate for meetings. As usual, people were gathered there.

I saw a friend and I walked right toward her. And she said: "Oh, Gigi! You've covered your hair!"

I didn't know what to say. I just said: "Yeah."

She surprised me. She asked, "Are you making a political statement?"

I didn't expect that question! I was still so nervous. I answered very slowly: "Nooooo. No, I'm not." That thought never even crossed my mind, I was only trying in my humble way to fulfill a spiritual desire that I had worked so hard to attain.

I suddenly realized: They're looking at me and they're wondering why I've just made this change. This was when the memory of 9/11 was still fresh in everyone's mind. So many things ran through my mind. Then, I just began to talk to my friend. I described the Hajj and what it meant to me. I explained to her how it was a spiritual rejuvenation and how I felt so much closer to my Creator during this time. I explained how I felt a sense of calm, peace and happiness upon my return. She listened.

We were friends—so she listened. And we remained good friends after that, because she was open. I remember that: She listened to my story. My life has changed since I began to wear the headscarf. Life does get a little bit harder when you decide to do this. You do have to keep wondering: Am I representing my faith properly? I know I'm just one person, but I do feel the weight of this commitment of wearing a visible sign that I am a part of the Muslim community.

I explain this to young women that, once you put on the scarf, your life does change. When people see you out in public, if you make a bad impression out there like you're rude to someone—well, the people who might see that misbehavior in public don't think: Oh, there's a rude woman. Because of the headscarf, they think: Oh, there's a rude Muslim!

This is a life-changing decision. It is a real responsibility to be a Muslim in America. I can't believe that it has been six years since the Hajj. A lot has happened over that time, but a lot is still the same. I still volunteer at school and in my community. I have taken a greater role in publicly representing the beauty of my faith—to correct the many common misconceptions about Islam.

My relationship with my Creator has grown stronger and has given me the inner peace I need to get through life. My headscarf is just another step in my spiritual journey.

CHAPTER 12

Padma Kuppa

Sharing Religious Ideals, American Ideals

When we are at our best as people, we are able to see our communities and our world as a loving family.

Padma is a community activist on behalf of diversity and education, especially in the areas of faith and culture. She was born in 1965 in India, moved to the United States as a child and grew up in a home where education was highly valued. As an adult, she has worked as an information technology consultant and also actively supports the Hindu temple in Troy, a city north of Detroit. After a lifetime as a proud American herself, Padma was surprised by one of her first public encounters with American neighbors of other faiths.

One of my favorite Bible verses is from 1 Corinthians: "Faith, hope and love abide, these three; and the greatest of these is love." This is a lot like passages in Hindu scriptures, including these words from the Maha Upanishad: "The whole world is a family." There also is a prayer of peace in the Rig Veda that reads, in English: "May all be happy. May all be healthy. May all be prosperous. Let no one suffer."

I'm a mom in a "typical" American family—like millions of other families in our country. We share common hopes for a happy, healthy life. My husband is an automotive engineer. My kids play baseball and soccer. My daughter has been a Girl Scout; my son has been a Cub Scout.

I try to serve my community as well as my own house of worship. A number of years ago, I agreed to serve on Troy's Ethnic Issues Advisory Board, a group of 10 people appointed by the City Council. That's one of the reasons I got involved in the National Day of Prayer.

When I first heard about Troy's annual public gathering for the annual National Day of Prayer event in 2004, I didn't know much about its history, but the idea of joining in prayer once a year sounded great to me. I didn't want to serve as the Hindu representative. I just hoped that the organizers would call the Hindu temple and invite someone who could represent our faith among all the other faiths that would be represented on the steps of City Hall that day. If they needed help finding someone, I was happy to ask around. I know quite a few people in the Hindu community.

But, as it turned out, no one called our temple. I was told that all the details for the Troy event in 2004 were already planned. I began to realize that there was no place in the Troy schedule for a Hindu to pray: we were being denied the right to participate in a program of prayer right there, on the steps of our own City Hall.

I sent an email to the City Council, expressing my concern about this. As a result, the mayor called me and said, "Padma, you can come and, during my opening remarks, you can say a Hindu prayer."

She was very welcoming to me that day, and said to the crowd of about 100 men, women and children: "Now, someone from our Ethnic Issues Advisory Board will say a few words."

From my place—standing beside the mayor—I slowly stepped over to the microphone. I was anxious to be addressing a crowd and, as I began to pray, I was so focused on the prayer itself that I wasn't focusing too much on the faces of the people standing in front of me. I simply used the four-line peace prayer from the Rig Veda. I recited it in Sanskrit and then in English. I didn't invoke any name. I didn't say, "Let's pray in the name of X, Y or Z." I just used the four simple lines of a prayer that people everywhere should be able to share.

But, as I stepped back, I could sense that most of the people didn't really want me there. I recall a Baha'i friend trying to reassure me with supportive words, but it became clear that this crowd didn't like my being there. I didn't leave after my prayer was finished. I participated in the whole program, which took about an hour. When the group prayed the Lord's Prayer, I prayed along.

As I talked with a few people afterward, I began to realize that this crowd was made up mainly of conservative Christians. Some of the children who attended the event were home-schooled. People were passing out literature from evangelical groups.

Finally, I thought: Boy, I shouldn't have come here today. I felt out of place and alone. I didn't realize that such opposition existed in my own community to people of other faiths.

I'm not naïve. I've always known that Michigan isn't as inclusive a place as my native New York. I still remember walking up to a counter at a place of business in Troy when a blonde, Caucasian woman walked up shortly after I got there. The person behind the counter turned to this woman and, without even acknowledging me, began to take care of her business first. Another time, my daughter wasn't invited to the birthday party of a good friend from school because this friend had chosen a Vacation Bible School theme for her party. My daughter was hurt that her friends had excluded her.

But it wasn't until 2005 that I realized how much some people in my own community hate the idea of allowing people of other faiths to take part in public events. I support our American ideals of freedom of speech and freedom of religion. We don't have to allow everyone into our houses of worship. We're free to express ourselves and our different faiths. But when someone plans to use a public place like the steps of City Hall for an official event that claims to represent our government and our whole community—that's different.

At first—in the months before that 2005 National Day of Prayer—I tried to get involved in the planning process for the event. Then, in March of that year, one City Council meeting got very ugly when the issue of diversity at these events was raised. As often happens with this kind of heated political issue, some activists from outside of our city had been brought in to try to argue the case for keeping a limitation on the National Day of Prayer.

I will never forget the experience of a man from an outside legal-advocacy center standing up and yelling at me—right there in my own hometown. He made me feel so little! He spoke to me as if to say: Why can't we crush you, this little bug, under our feet? I was stunned. I thought: If God created all of us, how can someone ever treat another human like that in God's name? You don't have to accept my beliefs. I don't have to accept your beliefs. But why can't we add our good wishes together, if we're going to share our prayers for the whole city? How could this man get so angry that he would treat me so hatefully? America has many faiths and also people of no faith, as well. All of us should feel welcome where we live.

In Troy, I hit a brick wall with this National Day of Prayer organization. At first, I didn't realize how closely its history is associated with conservative Christian political movements. At one point in 2005, I went online and got involved in an Internet chat with James Towey, the head of the office of faith-based initiatives for President George Bush. I asked Mr. Towey how President Bush observes the National Day of Prayer, and he said, "Oh, the President does it in a very diverse way!" And he pointed me to this document I could print out that showed how the White House includes many faiths in its observance. I thought that the document was the proof we needed to open things up in Troy. Everyone thought of President Bush as a conservative Christian, but he was inclusive in his expression of the National Day of Prayer.

Of course, nothing happened initially, in 2005. A long and complicated series of events unfolded that spring and, as a direct result, I became very active in helping to form a new organization, which is called the Troy Interfaith Group. That first spring, the Troy Interfaith Group had a diverse service that drew 250 people, including the city's mayor. She was threatened with a recall for supporting us, but that effort failed.

Since 2005, our group has grown and we have supported many programs that have inspired other people across the United States. In 2007, for example, our group was lifted up as an example by Harvard's Pluralism Project.

This whole journey started, for me, with my surprise in discovering that some of my neighbors did not want me to pray with them on the steps of our City Hall in the name of our City of Troy.

That's simply not the American ideal. When we are at our best as people, we are able to see our communities and our world as a loving family. I grew up celebrating holidays with friends of various faith traditions. When I was heading to college, my father gave me three books: the Bible, the Baghavad Gita and the complete works of William Shakespeare. He told me: "The world's great truths are in these three books."

I do believe there are certain truths all people can share— and one of them is that no one should make anyone else feel like "the other" in his or her own hometown. As a mom, I certainly don't want my children growing up feeling that way.

I realize that India isn't perfect in dealing with diversity. In India, people often are torn apart by socio-economic and religious stratification. America isn't perfect, either, but the United States is supposed to be a place in the world where everyone can be accepted for who he or she is. I'd be disappointed with myself if I *didn't* try to defend that American ideal. And although I may sound like a red-white-and-blue flag waver, I don't think that's such a bad thing if it helps us to remember who we're supposed to be in the world.

Part IV

Not Enemies
After All

CHAPTER 13

Motoko F. Huthwaite

Views From the Enemy Camps

When the sirens went off again, we all went and sat in the air raid shelter expecting to die there. There was no stopping the atomic bombs if they hit.

In this section of the book, women are telling stories about mistaken impressions of people—fearing that someone might be an enemy. Motoko's story turns the perspective 180 degrees. While still a girl, she experienced the suspicion and enmity of two nations. Born in Boston in 1927, Motoko's lifelong pursuit of education eventually led, in the 1970s, to a doctorate and professional expertise in children's literature. She remains deeply concerned about the quality of life for children and families around the world. She is a vigorous activist on behalf of ending nuclear weapons, promoting world peace and improving interfaith relations through her own lay leadership in the Presbyterian Church (USA).

I lived in America when Pearl Harbor was attacked. So, in December 1941, I was perceived as the enemy in my hometown of Cambridge, Massachusetts.

I lived in Japan when the atomic bomb was dropped on Hiroshima—so, then, I was perceived as the enemy in my family's homeland, where my clothing, my language and even my particular style of wire-rimmed glasses made me stand out as the enemy—this time as one of the Americans who was dropping bombs.

I was an enemy in both of my countries.

When the war started in 1941, I was 14 years old and in the ninth grade. My father was an orthodontist who taught at Harvard. He had been living in the United States since the 1920s, but the Oriental Exclusion Act of 1924 prevented him from becoming an American citizen. I was born in the U.S. and so was my brother, who was in fourth grade, so we were both dual citizens of Japan and the U.S.

When news of the attack on Pearl Harbor came, only my brother and I were at home. We heard it first from a Japanese Harvard student who called the house. He asked for my parents. I told him they weren't home. Then, he said, "Japan and America are at war!"

I had no idea what to do. I called for my brother to come inside. We sat there, inside the house, until my parents came home.

When I told my parents the news, I remember them turning absolutely white. They were aghast. We turned on the radio and we were glued to the announcer's voice saying, over and over again, that Pearl Harbor had been attacked.

The big question in our household was: Do we go to school the next day?

My brother and I attended a small private school called Buckingham—and we did return to classes the next day. That school had an excellent program and I remember the principal said to the whole student body at an assembly: "There will be no war within the walls of this school."

My brother and I were the only Japanese children in the school. So everyone was looking at us.

The principal also talked individually to children who were our friends, and they understood that they needed to protect us. My best friends would sit in a circle around me. And my brother was surrounded by his friends at recess. One of his friends told other boys, quite loudly: "You touch him and I'll knock yer block off!"

But school wasn't the only place we had to go outside our home. Each week, I had to take a bus across the Charles River into Boston to my piano lesson. The first time I had to do that I sat there, so frightened, in my seat on the bus: If they realize that I am Japanese, what will they do to me? I wondered. And I worked out a plan in my head: If someone confronts me, I'll tell them I'm Chinese. They won't know the difference. But, there was no problem on the bus.

My parents faced far worse problems. One day, the police accosted my mother, claiming she was taking a photograph of a bridge; they had mistaken her rectangular-shaped purse for a camera. Then, my parents came home another day with funny stains on their fingers because they had been fingerprinted. The Japanese students at Harvard were in trouble. Some of my father's patients cancelled.

We got a telegram from the U.S. government that said: If you desire repatriation to Japan, report to Ellis Island at such-and-such a date. My parents carefully considered this, and they decided we were no longer welcome in the U.S. My father decided that he would stay and continue his dental practice and keep our apartment, but that my mother, my brother and I would go to Japan.

Do you know who stepped forward to help us at this very difficult time? Quakers. We were Buddhist and Shinto, like most Japanese families, and so I was absolutely bewildered to meet these people who called themselves Quakers. When other people were trying to kick us out of our apartment and were refusing to allow my mother to shop in their stores—the Quakers came and befriended us. They even escorted us to Ellis Island to make sure we were safe.

In 1942, we moved to Tokyo. We stayed with my aunt, my mother's oldest sister. We had lots of family in Japan—aunts and uncles and cousins. I went to an international school run by the Convent of the Sacred Heart and was taught by nuns. My brother and I could speak and understand Japanese, but we were terrible at reading and writing the language. Fortunately our instruction, at first, was in English.

Then the war got worse, and we weren't allowed to speak English: It was the enemy language. I stood out wherever I went because my clothes were so obviously American. We knew that people were watching us. We could go outside in the morning and find boot prints in the dirt: places where the secret police had stood near our windows at night, listening to what we were saying in the house.

Once again, friends from school were so important. But we had to be careful wherever we went. One day, a friend and I forgot and began speaking English on a public street. The principal called us into the office and said that we should never do that again! We were speaking the enemy language. It was dangerous.

As the war went on and the Americans got closer to Japan, there was first a campaign with incendiary bombs that was devastating to some Japanese cities, where the homes burned easily. At least during the firebombing, there was something we could do: we could join a bucket brigade to put out fires. I remember one woman stood up on her roof, sweeping cinders away with a broom.

But nothing could be done about these atomic bombs that could wipe out an entire city with a single blast. After the news of the first atomic bomb—and when the sirens went off again—we all went and sat in the air raid shelter, expecting to die right there.

Finally, the war ended and I was forced to choose a citizenship. If I chose to become Japanese, I would never see my American friends again. If I chose to become American, I would hurt my Japanese family members and friends. In the end, I chose to become an American because English was my language and the U.S. was the place where I had the greatest chance of completing my education and becoming independent.

I got a job working for the Allied Occupation of Japan, where I could earn money to pay for my passage back to the U.S. Then I enrolled at Radcliffe, and worked my way through college by looking after children for professors and other families.

What I remember most about the whole experience was the importance of friends, the surprise of these Quaker people who befriended us—and how doubly wonderful peace felt when the war was over!

Getting in touch with friends again after the war was absolute heaven!

The world seemed to begin again.

CHAPTER 14

Judy Goddard Satterthwaite

Melting the Cold War

The beauty of the times we had just shared made her startling revelation a minor piece of who she had become in my eyes.

Judy is an industrial consultant living in southeast Michigan. As a child, she was raised a Christian Scientist, which she says helps her focus on the positive aspects of life—and of the people she meets. Growing up in a religious minority also gave her an appreciation for others who are in the minority. Judy believes that being different can be good if one is willing to accept and love oneself, and others, as cherished children of God. Although she eventually left the Christian Science Church, Judy believes that the foundation of unconditional love has greatly influenced her life.

About 20 years ago, a Russian professor from Kiev named Valerie Kadyrov contacted me and asked if I would be interested in selling his product in the United States. Having been in sales for a while, I already knew that I loved to converse and mingle with others. I told him that I would be more than happy to help sell his product.

I ended up visiting Kiev, Ukraine, in December 1991. I wanted to see the product I would be selling—which was, in fact, a detonation coating process—in operation, so that I could better explain and sell the idea to customers in the U.S. I also brought a cash advance from another partner in the U.S. so that the Kadyrov family would have some money to work with.

My visit occurred just after the Soviet Union was dissolved, and it was quite apparent that the economy was struggling. I stayed with Valerie Kadyrov and his wife, Ludmila, in their apartment. Valerie's son, Erik, was studying advanced physics at the University of Wisconsin and was hoping to work on a superconductor. When I arrived in Kiev, their daughter moved in with a friend temporarily so that I could stay in her room.

Professor Kadyrov was one of the 5,000 Ph.D.s working at the Institute of Materials Sciences in Kiev—he was part of the Russian "brain trust" living in that city. At the collapse of the Soviet Union, the institute had no money. As a result, many of the scientists who had salable projects were trying to market them in whatever way they could. There were many other technical advances developed at the institute in addition to the coating process that Valerie was trying to market to the U.S. During a tour of the facilities, I saw a fabric of Basalt rock, made by melting the rock and forming it into a fine hollow thread that was then woven into a silky fabric. There was a demonstration of new welding processes—glass to metal (very new at the time)—and several other advances in materials applications.

The Kadyrov home was a modest, two-bedroom apartment. The hallways were dark and we always walked up the stairs to their floor because electricity was at a premium. They had put up and decorated a small Christmas tree for me in their sitting room. During the course of my visit, Ludmila took me to see the art museum, a beautiful church, and displays of miniatures and historical artifacts. At the museum, the lights were turned on when visitors entered a room and quickly turned off as soon as they moved on. Heat was kept at a minimum. I was especially intrigued by the fact that Ukraine had new currency—but no coins! As a result, all the pay phones in the city were free. People were expected to "take turns" using the phones so all could make their calls as needed. Ludmila was determined that I see the beauty and culture of Kiev, while Valerie insisted I visit the war museum, which was fronted by a statue that paid tribute to victory and Russian MiG planes.

Both of the Kadyrovs were very concerned for my safety. I was never to go out alone! Even when I ventured out with Ludmila, Valerie suggested that I wear one of her coats so I didn't look so "Western." I would spend evenings telling Ludmila about my sons and my life in America. She understood more English than I did Russian. I learned how to say "okay" in Russian—we both said that word a lot!

Ludmila and Valerie were also intent upon showing me a pleasant time, so we ate at an ice cream parlor and went to a circus. Valerie's daughter and her boyfriend took me to see a performance of *Romeo and Juliet* by the Russian Ballet Theater at the Kiev Opera House. Money and goods were very scarce, so I appreciated all they did to make me feel welcome.

The last evening, Ludmila and I shopped for groceries. She struggled mightily with a decision to buy (or not buy) a cake for dessert. In the end, she left me at the car and ran back to the bakery to get the cake for my last dinner with them. I expressed my wonder, which bordered on awe, at all that she was able to do to care for her family under such difficult circumstances. That's when she told me that she was used to hardships and difficulties—years before, when her children were small, they lived in a secure village in the Ural Mountains where she had worked as a nuclear scientist. In fact, she had traveled to Cuba and other countries around the world, to help with the installation of nuclear weapons facilities for the Communist government! I was, at first, both surprised and stunned. However, the beauty of the times we had just shared made her startling revelation a minor piece of who she had become in my eyes. She was Ludmila, the gentle soul who was a gracious hostess under difficult circumstances, who laughed with me and cried with me, and struggled to speak some English to me when I could speak very little Russian.

The sweet little blond woman who had opened her home and her heart to me was one of the Russian nuclear scientists that we, in the West, had pictured as demonic monsters! She was no monster—she was a loving wife to her husband, a mom who worried about her kids and someone who had welcomed a visitor from the United States into her home, demonstrating a truly warm heart.

If we are willing to be open to others—to listen and learn and share—we will find many more similarities than differences. Even though languages and circumstances may separate us, hearts can unite us.

CHAPTER 15

Shari Rogers
Opening Doors, Opening Eyes, Opening Hearts

Together, we can create unity in place of isolation, trust in place of fear, and love in place of misunderstanding.

Shari is a psychologist who is active in Jewish organizations and, now in her 40s, is devoting more time to studying the religious teachings and traditions of Judaism. Through religious study, her larger assumptions about the world are expanding. Specifically, her study of Torah has enhanced both her understanding of herself and of all relationships. One of her first interreligious encounters enlarged her awareness in a surprising way.

I grew up in a home where intellectual life and appreciation of all cultures was celebrated. My parents were both master's-level Bridge players who enjoyed Bridge three nights a week with people from many different backgrounds. They were very open in the friendships they formed, as well as in their intellectual interests. Our family traveled extensively around the world, thus giving me a comfort level with all people.

My education in Judaism began at Jewish Day School and culminated sadly with my Bat Mitzvah. But it was my sister Darra's increasing religious observance during adulthood that sparked my interest in learning both the Torah and the Jewish studies that I have pursued during the past decade. In addition, I received my doctorate in clinical psychology, where I was trained in the psychoanalytic model. As much as I respect using psychoanalytic principles in helping other people to achieve personal growth, they have their limitations. I believe that the tenets of Judaism have at least as much—if not more—potential to enhance a person's life.

I remember visiting the Holocaust museum in Jerusalem. One particular insight from my guide remains with me to this day: He said that intellect alone—without a heart and soul, without a moral center to our lives—is not enough in this world. He pointed out that in the 1930s, many of the people who joined the Nazi party were very well-educated and culturally sophisticated people—doctors, artists, musicians and educators—and they still fell under the spell of Hitler's words. As the guide spoke of his experiences that day, it became clear to me that the vast intellectual and scientific accomplishments the world has seen in the last few decades will not serve as a deterrent to injustice, hatred and intolerance.

In my recent studies of Judaism, I have come to understand why one of the most important tenets is *Tikkun Olam* (rectification of the world) because the Torah recognizes that every human being has to battle to overcome negative character traits within him- or herself. Every person has a destructive potential within. Therefore, the goal is to first recognize this, and to engage in a struggle with self, and then to use free will to change this negative potential. The outcome of this struggle will help the individual to be kinder in thoughts, words and actions, and the world becomes a better place. If we fail to do this and if we let our nature control us, it becomes possible for the brightest and most cultured individuals to perpetrate the worst crimes in the history of humanity

My friend Brenda Rosenberg is very involved in interfaith groups like WISDOM and in projects like "Reuniting the Children of Abraham." She is always trying to bring people together, across their individual boundary lines. When she knew that I was getting more deeply involved in religious studies, she invited me to go with her to an international conference called "ENGAGING the OTHER" that was held at Oakland University. I found it fascinating to meet so many people—especially Muslim clerics and Arab community leaders from as far away as Saudi Arabia—who were willing to be in a space that focused on creating understanding.

Next, Brenda invited me to visit a mosque; her friend Hind Kabawat, a peace activist from Syria, flew in to be part of the program. This was a mosque that most Jews never visit. We knew that a large crowd was expected, but were shocked to find that 900 people were in attendance. I must admit, I was apprehensive. I questioned whether or not I should really be in a mosque. Was I betraying my faith? Some of my other friends voiced their concerns. They told me I was absolutely insane for doing this. They were afraid for my safety.

We walked into this mosque, covering our heads with scarves in respect for the Muslims' traditions. This wasn't awkward for me. I am aware of the importance of covering one's head to communicate modesty. My sister is an observant Jew who dresses modestly and covers her hair. I was touched by the similarity.

We were warmly greeted. Brenda knew so many people, and you could sense that, with these people, she had real friendships; she even received hugs from most of the women.

As we were ushered to a front table, next to the key dignitaries and speakers, a woman sitting next to me leaned over and said: "You look very familiar to me!"

I thought: What is she thinking? She must be mistaking me for someone else.

Then she said, "Oh, I know you!"

I knew that wasn't possible.

When she mentioned my parents' names, I was flabbergasted. This woman in a mosque knows my parents' names? How could she know?

"Through Bridge," she continued. "We were friends with your parents. Are they still playing Bridge?"

I sat there, stunned. But she was already inquiring about the welfare of my various family members. Suddenly here I was, in the middle of this mosque, catching up on all the latest family news with this Muslim woman.

The experience was eye-opening. My fears and the fears of my friends had sullied what I had prided myself on most: being an open, empathic person who likes to connect to people.

This woman's connection to my family members shattered the glass that seemed to separate us. We had so much more in common than our appearances might suggest, and even more to share and give if we could only reach through that new opening between us.

In times when religion and cultural values are distorted to justify hatred and dissension, wouldn't it be amazing if, instead, we could open new doors to kindness and love of humanity? Together, we can create unity in place of isolation, trust in place of fear, and love in place of misunderstanding. If each person does what they can to open doors, we will surely see *Tikkun Olam*—a world repaired, a world at peace.

CHAPTER 16

Sheri Schiff

When People Change

He had a fit, an absolute fit. ... My boss said I had deceived him.

By training, Sheri is an educator. By nature, she's always been a front-line, first-person advocate for equality and opportunity for all. She's trained others in anti-bias and multi-cultural education. Sheri is a leader in her Jewish community, a docent for the Holocaust Memorial Center in Farmington Hills, Michigan, and a member of outreach groups such as WISDOM. Because of her compassion, courage and convictions, she has built personal connections across racial, cultural and religious boundaries.

I cannot remember the first time I met a person from another race or religion or ethnic group because I grew up in a fairly diverse neighborhood in Detroit. My childhood friends were Italian, African-American and Jewish. But there were so many rules in each family; in my family, I could not make friends unless they were high achievers in school.

I am a second-generation American who grew up in an observant Jewish home. My grandparents came to this country fleeing pogroms in Russia. After my parents divorced—when I was around 3 years old—my grandmother raised me while my mother went to work. I lived with my grandmother, mother, aunt and uncle and spent lots of time with my great-aunts and great-uncles, as well as my great-grandmother—my *bubbe*.

Everyone in the neighborhood knew a little Yiddish, a little Italian and some of the black-American colloquialisms. Both my grandmother and our African-American neighbors raised chickens in our backyards. We exchanged chicken recipes, but not the food: Ours were slaughtered kosher. I ate only kosher food or kosher-style food.

I jumped double-dutch with the girl next door, but was not allowed to eat in her house—although she always ate in ours. Her mom kept cookies with a *Cheksher*—a kosher seal—in the house, so that I could have a snack there.

I was allowed to go to my black neighbor's church, but not the Italian neighbor's Catholic church.

I was told, as a child, that if I had a problem or needed help that I should ask a black person. My family trusted our Italian neighbors, but made sure that I stayed out of their Catholic churches because they were afraid that I would be seized by the church and baptized against my will. Their paranoia was due to the difficulties they had experienced as Jews in Russia and as immigrants when they came to America.

I was arrested for civil rights protests for the first time when I was 15 at a segregated swimming pool in Detroit. My grandmother and uncle bailed me out of jail. I remember my Grandmother Rose speaking Yiddish to the judge—who understood her telling him she wouldn't punish me for standing up to discrimination.

My personal hero is my Grandmother Rose—may she rest in peace. Rose Kallman Bakst was a courageous woman who walked out of Eastern Europe, made peace with a brutal situation, survived a pogrom and lived her life with dignity and grace. She was not schooled, but was fluent in English, Yiddish, Russian and Polish—all spoken with an Eastern European accent. She stood up to injustice and taught me the saying that I live by: "Justice, justice, you shall pursue."

When I was at Michigan State University for my graduate assistantship in the Department of Communications, I worked in the cooperative extension service doing drug-education work. My boss thought I was Italian, because my last name was Terebelo: That name reflected my adopted father's family, which was Italian Jewish.

My boss invited me to his home for dinner one night. There I was, at the dinner table, and I looked down at my plate; the main course that night was ham.

I took one look at the ham and said to myself : I'm not going to break *kashrut*—Hebrew for kosher—for him.

You know when you sometimes shove food around your plate to make it look like you're eating? That's what I was doing. Well, his mother-in-law—who made the ham—noticed I wasn't eating. My boss noticed too, and I said that I wasn't really hungry, but he would not let it go.

Finally, I told him it wasn't part of my diet, that I was Jewish and that I kept kosher.

He had a fit, an absolute fit. His mother started talking about fumigating the chairs. His kids started talking about Jews killing Jesus. My boss said I had deceived him.

After that, I had a tough time at work. My boss reassigned me to a high school in an area of Michigan known for being home to local leaders of the Ku Klux Klan. I came into my office one day and there was a noose in there. Once, as I was driving in the area, I thought I was headed into a nice sunset—and soon realized it was a burning cross.

That was my trial by fire: surviving my work there.

But the story doesn't end there. In the early 1990s, one young man prompted change. He was a graduate of that same high school who went off to the University of Michigan where he found that his randomly assigned roommate was African-American. This roommate was a graduate of one of the Detroit area's most rigorous prep schools, but the white student was enraged at the living situation. He failed in an attempt to get another roommate and, instead, divided the room with a piece of tape. But one night, when the white student was stuck over a math problem, his black roommate offered advice on how to get the answer. The white student begrudgingly thanked him. The line down the middle of the room faded a bit. Another night, the black student invited his roommate to have dinner with his buddies. Little by little, the white student found his racist beliefs shattered simply by getting to know his roommate.

This white student carried that personal transformation further. He went back to his old school and demanded that administrators and teachers change. They agreed to try to start teaching differently. And, that has prompted my own reconnection with these schools. I was invited to facilitate workshops and help revise teaching materials. Twenty years had passed since my first encounters with racism, but I was witnessing that change is possible even in such tough situations.

I know how complex it can be to navigate relationships in a diverse world. I've lived with these issues all my life. But

I've also taught people how to make the changes that can welcome a more diverse society.

Entire communities can change—but it takes people to spark that transformation.

CHAPTER 17

The Rev. Sharon Buttry

From Conflict in the Streets to Healing Waters

> *The biggest surprise for me in this very difficult experience was how much there is in common among the Abrahamic traditions.*

Rev. Sharon is a Baptist pastor who works in cross-cultural urban ministry. Her ministry ranges from working with educational groups to leading retreats to activating peace in a way that trains and empowers society's most vulnerable people.

I don't think of the Kingdom of God in the hereafter. I think of it as something that is possible now.

In Ezekiel, we have the biblical image of the healing of nations that begins with water flowing from the sanctuary of God, spreading out across the land, bringing its healing power to all it touches. The work that I do—advocating for and teaching self-advocacy to those who are disenfranchised within their own communities—often feels like rowing against the stream. It can be very challenging to bring people together to work in a common direction. It's difficult to change a culture of conflict in which people define themselves by their differences, rather than by their common human experiences. But then there are other times when it all comes together in fellowship; you can almost feel the current of a community united around truth and a cause carrying you forward.

I like to say that I was born in a cornfield east of Columbus, Ohio, and grew up in farmland. I wasn't really born in a field, of course, but it was an isolated, rural area and such a contrast to the asphalt and concrete that surrounds my home these days. As I grew up, my Protestant family was very involved in the church. My dad was a lay preacher—not theologically trained—but the church was the center of our lives. Every Saturday, it seemed, we cleaned the church, and when we weren't doing that, we were there doing other activities. My mother was very service-oriented as well, visiting the sick and writing letters for the blind in nursing homes. In our church, 13 was the age of accountability, and I went through a passage of baptism, making a serious commitment to faith at that time in my life.

I was 19 when I married my husband. He was the son of an American Baptist Air Force chaplain and we decided that our purpose as a couple was to put God first in our lives. He went to seminary and became a pastor and is now working in international peace and justice work. I earned a Master's of Divinity, too—the master's degree that prepares clergy for ministry—and I also earned a Master's in Social Work, so today I am both an American Baptist pastor and a licensed master social worker. That training equipped me to fully join my husband in dedicating our lives to serving others and in bringing about peace and justice. For us it is centered in Christian theology—Jesus laid down His life in love for people, and that's a model we take very seriously. He taught love of one's enemies, which is a unique teaching—the idea that you can embrace and clothe and feed your enemy. Reconciliation is a very powerful force in our theology. It's been a wonderful journey.

My job brought us to the Detroit area. My goal was to work in disenfranchised communities and to give voice, especially, to youth and to those people who are most vulnerable in American culture and society. From 1996–2005, I directed a nonprofit social service center for the American Baptist Church, and then, in 2005, I partnered with Pastor John Myers, who started ACTS 29 Fellowship. In this new work, our model was to meet physical, emotional and social needs; that's the kind of work I was doing the first nine years. But in ACTS 29, we now also pay close attention to spiritual needs and provide opportunities for spiritual growth for all ages in a worshiping community.

The Fellowship has grown out of the people who've been touched by the ministries: We now have a construction team that does home repair; we teach English as a second language; we reach out to kids through summer camping and backpacking, in Michigan and in other states. Each time we grow I think of Ezekiel and those waters flowing from the Sanctuary of God, bringing healing to the nations.

There are rough waters, too, in this kind of work! In 2004, we faced a major problem in Hamtramck, the small city where I work, and where there is a large Muslim population living among a shrinking Polish-Catholic population. One of the growing mosques wanted to broadcast its call to prayer over loudspeakers to the surrounding neighborhood, much like mosques do in Muslim communities around the world. Leaders of this mosque asked the City Council for guidance on moving forward in a way that would be in keeping with local ordinances. The City Council reviewed the sound ordinance and realized that an amendment would be required that would recognize this kind of outdoor use of loudspeakers for congregations. This became a much larger issue, because it turned out that local Catholic churches had been broadcasting musical calls to prayer that were in violation of the existing ordinance. The amendment essentially would have permitted all the houses of worship to do this. Working with the imam to try to resolve this problem was my first interfaith experience as an adult.

Some people rose up against the idea of allowing a mosque to make its public call to prayer. In fact, some opposition groups came into Hamtramck from other parts of the country to protest. Before the issue was resolved, news reporters came from all over the world, and some confrontations were tense—especially in the streets with some of the protest groups.

I worked with a group of Muslim and Christian leaders who simply pointed out that these religious expressions from congregations were consistent with the Constitution. We tried to dispel stereotypes. We wove new interfaith partnerships. We began a Hamtramck interfaith clergy group, which included Jewish participation as well.

The biggest surprise for me in this very difficult experience was how much there is in common among the Abrahamic traditions: Judaism, Christianity and Islam.

In this case, we were working specifically with Christians and Muslims, and it was fun for me to help people from many different backgrounds see that these two faiths that seemed to be at odds actually share important truths that we believe make a difference beyond this life. The imam and I were very open about our traditions' propensities to proselytize and, once that was out in the open, we could say: "I know I am not going to convert you, but we still can be friends and find common ground and plenty of things to do together to make our community a more upright place."

How wonderful it would sound if that was the end of my story, with hands clasped across differences. But this is truly the story of a flow of water—a river of relationships that keeps flowing and changing. Sometimes, we don't agree on where this water should be taking us.

In 2008, religious groups once again got involved in a local political struggle. This time, the confrontation involved a proposed human rights ordinance in an effort to broadly prohibit discrimination in housing, employment and public accommodations; and this time, the ordinance included sexual orientation. New attitudes surfaced, including the biases of some outsiders who came into our town and challenged the ordinance. Opponents of these proposed civil-rights protections gathered enough signatures to place the proposed ordinance on a local ballot, assuming they could defeat the idea this way.

My husband and I worked tirelessly to promote the idea that all people deserve the chance to live and work where they want, even if their sexual orientation is different from our own.

This time around, our good friends in the Muslim community took up an opposing position on the ballot. It broke our hearts to hear the things people said against their neighbors. As happened with my earlier work on protecting the call to prayer, I met a whole new group of people in my community; we had never crossed paths until this new effort arose in our community.

As I worked to build support for the ordinance, my friend the imam called me and—this time—he raked me over the coals for supporting the ordinance. In this case, the ballot initiative failed and the human-rights ordinance was lost.

But, my friendship with the imam remains, I hope. We have met since the ballot initiative. I don't believe that our relationship, forged in the heat of community activism in support of Muslim neighbors, was just utilitarian on his part. It was genuine and I hope we will get back to working together again.

Part of what fuels my hope is the vision of our community, someday, as a jewel of diversity and peace—the kind of community where others will want to live as well. But the only way to make that vision a reality is by working through our faith traditions. We need to transform character in the very places where character has become destructive and violent in its expression.

The healing waters described in Ezekiel have no end because they flow from God's sanctuary. The waters, like God's love, are endless. That's what gives me hope. That's what keeps me working to bring God's Kingdom to the here and now.

Part V

Weaving
Creative Ideas

CHAPTER 18

Edith Broida
Forming a Group of Explorers

If there is one thing that every group has in common, it's that it has experienced suffering. Maybe, if we learn more about how and why everyone has suffered, it would make all of us more compassionate.

Edith is a graduate of Wayne State University who began her teaching career in 1958 and retired from the profession 35 years later. Her religious beliefs vary, but she is a devoted member of both Temple Israel, which is a Reform Jewish temple, and the Birmingham Temple, which is a Humanistic Judaism congregation. An avid reader and current facilitator of book groups, Edith's choice of readings reflects her interest in different cultures and different faiths. Her interest in history led to the formation of The Museum Group, which offered more opportunities to learn about the beliefs of others.

My earliest memory of an interfaith/intercultural experience was when I was in the eighth grade. I had a great friend whose name was Connie, and she and I would talk about our differences; I was Jewish, and she was Greek Orthodox. This was after World War II, and everyone at that time was very conscious of being *American*. America was a melting pot, and Connie and I decided we would go to each other's church and synagogue.

I remember sitting there—the church was so new that there was still sawdust in the lobby—and suddenly, I smelled something. I leaned over to Connie and said, "Oh, no! I think the church is on fire!" She looked at her mother, and they smiled at each other: What I was smelling was incense! It just shows how we don't know much about each other's faiths, and how useful it would be to know more.

I went to a mostly Jewish high school until, in the tenth grade, my family moved to a blue-collar neighborhood. Suddenly I was different, and people would say things that they didn't know were demeaning to me. But my parents had moved a lot—seven times in my 12 years of school—so I was used to being different. At Wayne State University I joined a Jewish sorority, and later, I married a Jewish man.

Many years later, when an Arab-American Museum opened in Michigan, I came up with the idea of The Museum Group. I thought: We already have the Charles Wright African-American Museum and the Holocaust Museum in the Metro Detroit area. What would happen if I gathered a diverse group, and we would all go to one another's museums? With Deborah Smith-Pollard, an African-American woman, and Renee Ahee, a Lebanese-American woman, we formed The Museum Group. It wasn't Jews with Jews, blacks with blacks or Arabs with Arabs; we were all together.

In all three museums, we found an emphasis on American history—how the people came to America, and what they achieved. But if there is one thing that every group has in common, it's that it has experienced suffering. Maybe, if we learn more about how and why everyone has suffered, it would make all of us more compassionate.

At the Charles Wright Museum, we learned that when Africans were put onto the slave ships, they were given salt pork—a food staple that was so different from that in their regular diet that many of them died. The museum even had a simulation of a slave ship rocking, and we could hear moaning. It gave us a good idea of what it might have been like to be a slave.

After visiting the Charles Wright Museum, we went out to eat, which was our practice—this time at Ruby's Kitchen on Woodward, where we ate fried chicken, mashed potatoes and gravy. After all of our museum explorations, we ate ethnic food and allowed time to talk.

The Museum Group grew, and some, unknowingly, said things that ruffled feathers. Knowing this, I held a meeting at my house. I was disturbed that people were becoming uncomfortable with one another. As we talked and shared our feelings—becoming quite emotional—we said that if *we* can't get along, there's no hope for the rest of the world! We were now far more sensitive to how people felt, and the following year, we decided that it wasn't just our ethnic backgrounds that made us who we were, but also our religious backgrounds. We decided we should also visit one another's place of worship.

First, we went to a Lebanese-Christian church, and there, I was surprised that the services weren't that different from my own Jewish services. We then went to a church in Detroit, and it was great, with everyone dressed up and singing joyously. The pastor met with us afterward and arranged a brunch with hummus, bagels—food that he thought would be pleasing to all of us. We also went to an evening service at my temple. What I noticed was that the religious leaders in each of these places went out of their way to make us feel welcome.

I once read an article in *Real Simple* magazine, an interview with women who were 100 years old or older. In this article, one woman said, "If there is a God, he is the God of everyone." And I thought: How true and logical this is. No one—whether Islamic imam or Catholic priest or Orthodox rabbi—can possibly own God. My temple has even taken out pronouns that refer to God as "Him." I liked this elderly woman's wise statement because it really spoke to a universal God.

Since most of the women in The Museum Group are professionals or traveling retirees, it's often hard for us to get together. Forming such a group is a challenge, but we have learned how valuable it is to visit historical museums and religious institutions together. We discover that we're not as different as we think!

In America, millions of immigrants did not know English when they arrived; they encountered prejudice; they faced enormous challenges; this is such a widespread story for so many families. Millions began here, in the U.S., as part of a first generation, learning the language and struggling through menial jobs—hoping to see that their children's lives would be better than their own.

I'd like to see our Museum Group become a model that is duplicated in school groups, PTAs, church groups, women's clubs and other organizations. Many of us have experienced great success in America. We need to learn our respective stories and broaden our world.

CHAPTER 19

The Rev. Charlotte H. Sommers

Connections Through a Death in the Family

As we form friendships, we discover there are things we all share in life—like concern for parents.

The Rev. Charlotte H. Sommers is the pastor at Northminster Presbyterian Church in Troy, Michigan, and convener of the Troy Interfaith Group. In the larger community, she works to promote diversity, and her latest accomplishment was working with the Troy Interfaith Group to create an Interfaith Labyrinth on the grounds of the Northminster Church. Labyrinths are not mazes intended to confuse the walker, but rather circular pathways that lead slowly but surely to a central point. Walking the labyrinth is a tool for prayer and meditation. The practice was developed centuries ago to blend prayer and movement, as in a pilgrimage. In her story, Charlotte talks about the vital relationships that form around such work.

In the Troy Interfaith Group, we commit ourselves to "invite people to gather, grow and give for the sake of promoting the common values of love, peace and justice among all religions locally and globally." We "believe that peace among peoples and nations requires peace among religions." —based on a statement by Hans Küng.

Our group hosts some major events during the year, and one of these is the National Day of Prayer, which we observe with an interfaith service. A few years ago in Troy, we had a controversy that made news headlines across the state. National Day of Prayer events are often supported by evangelical Christians, and here in Troy, a Hindu woman, Padma Kuppa, wanted to say a prayer in a public National Day of Prayer event, but was discouraged. This led a number of us to form the Troy Interfaith Group. I offered to host the Interfaith National Day of Prayer event at Northminster Church, where I am the pastor, which is how I got involved.

Now, there are several of us from the interfaith group who have lunch together every month. We just casually say it's time to get together for lunch and then we talk about all kinds of things, from books to politics to what's going on in our lives and our families. These friendships have developed as a result of working with the Troy Interfaith Group, which was a surprise to me; I didn't expect these deeper friendships to develop.

As we form friendships, we discover there are things we all share in life—like concern for parents. The first time I visited a Hindu friend's home for lunch, it was after she attended my mother's memorial service. I so appreciated her being there, and afterward, she invited me for lunch to talk about some things I had said in the service. As we shared that lunch, we talked about my parents, and we also talked about her parents. She told me that something I had said in the memorial service about my mother really impacted her. My mother had taught me that our feelings are not "right" or "wrong." Our feelings are real. We shouldn't try to correct or fix people's feelings. We shouldn't say, "Don't feel that way!" If we want to build good relationships, we should listen and not judge another person's feelings.

As our time together continued, this Hindu friend and I talked about all kinds of lessons we'd learned from our families. We talked about prayer. We talked about lots of things. It was wonderful.

There also were some Muslim women who called and said they wanted to come visit me after my mother died. They said this was part of their tradition; they visit with the person who is grieving. I was so moved by their thoughtfulness. It was a really wonderful thing to offer. Unfortunately, our schedules were such that we couldn't actually get together, but the fact that they wanted to come and visit with me was very meaningful. They weren't of the Christian tradition, but they were showing a sense of compassion—and they were showing me a traditional way that they expressed this compassion in their community. Their call and that idea inspired me.

These experiences have shown me that we need to spend more time together, talking with people of different traditions. We need to enlarge the circle of people who interact with one another. When the Troy Interfaith Group hosts an event like our National Day of Prayer service or our Interfaith Thanksgiving Day service, we are "preaching to the choir." Usually the people who attend are already on the bandwagon. It's the people who would never attend such an event that we are really trying to reach.

Closing off our lives—insulating ourselves from other faiths and cultures—is a dangerous choice. We can't escape the fact that we're a global community now. The more we learn about each other, the "healthier and wealthier" we all become.

CHAPTER 20

Paula Drewek
Journeys Toward Friendship

What I remember is that the experience started with sickness. … But, what an evening! What an evening!

Paula is Baha'i and a retired professor of humanities and comparative religions. Now she devotes much of her time to interfaith work and uses all that she has learned throughout her life to form new relationships and help

others. Over the past two decades, she has made many trips to India to spend time at the Barli Development Institute for Rural Women in Indore.

W hen you reach a certain point in life, you realize that many individuals have made a difference in shaping the person you have become. Among those people in my life is a couple I met in 1993 when I first visited India: Janak and Jimmy McGilligan. Janak is a former Hindu who became a Baha'i shortly before taking on a position at the Barli Development Institute for Rural Women. Jimmy is a Baha'i from Ireland who was doing some community work in India when they met and later decided to marry. I met them on my first visit to India when I was doing research for my doctorate and I have since been back every three years because I can't bear to *not* be in touch with these wonderful people.

When I first arrived, Janak and Jimmy met me at the airport and it was a delightful meeting; we met, we hugged and they welcomed me. I was like a dear sister who had come to learn about them and the Barli Institute—and, of course, I do dearly love the Institute now because of the work it's done and the many lives it's changed.

Together, Jimmy and Janak help to run the place: Jimmy manages the farm and land, and Janak takes care of the program and curricula. In my visits, I usually spend anywhere from two weeks to a month. Although it may seem like a remote place from our American perspective, I've been amazed at how often I've met people from around the world who have been to their doors. Myself and people from India, China, Britain, Australia, America, Sweden—we all funnel through this Institute because, since it was founded in 1986, it has grown and become very well-known in development circles.

The women of the Institute continue to give me joy every time I go. They are rural—from village life, from low castes, generally between the ages of 15 and 25 and they don't even know the local language of Hindi. Our means of communication are very limited to things that are visual and auditory, because language isn't an option. We dance together, we sing together, and they take such joy in the ordinary things of life, like listening to a piece of music and picking tamarind from a tree. One time when I was there, we made tamarind pickles and rolled out *papadums,* and to these women, every little task was just so much fun. They do all of their cooking with solar cookers; they raise all of their food on the three acres that are cultivated as part of this Institute.

The one thing I remember the most is from my earliest visit. There were a couple of trips we took to places outside of Barli and, in one case, we went to a village that was very remote—about four hours away. The man in that village who had been a Baha'i the longest had come right up to the door of the director's house to invite us to come and celebrate a holy day with his village. I had to ride in the back of a jeep for four hours over Indian roads and when I got there, I was carsick! But the people of this village were so welcoming.

We met outside, and they had a number of *charpoys*—traditional Indian beds made of woven strips in a wooden frame. They had brought these outside, arranged them around a fire and invited us to sit down. We did a lot of singing and we formed a procession around the village with big torches. After we had processioned through the whole village, we came to an area where they had an oven in the ground, where they were cooking bread balls. I'm not sure that I could have eaten the bread balls or drunk the water, so I ate what we had brought along—a few things like peanut butter and jelly and graham crackers. But that whole celebration with the people of that village— everyone seated on the ground, with the fire going at night—was so filled with spirit and love and the joy of being together. I will just never forget it.

What sticks out in my memory is that the experience started with sickness—I felt really yucky after that awful ride along bumpy roads. But, what an evening! What an evening!

So, the people in that village—and friends like Jimmy and Janak—continue to teach me about the spiritual principles of unity and how to relate to people of different cultures. I continue to learn from friends like these.

CHAPTER 21

Patty and Elana Haron

Bringing Diversity Into the Schools

You can call me Suzie Sunshine for talking like this. I've gotten burned plenty of times because of my outlook on life, but I remain optimistic.

Patty and Elana Haron are mother and daughter who have long enjoyed friendships that cross cultural and religious boundaries. Elana even started a diversity club at her high school. But a dramatic experience in Israel with other teenagers prompted Elana to re-evaluate relationships at her high school back home. She was determined to help more people form cross-cultural friendships. Soon her mother, Patty, got involved in the project, too.

Elana's Story:

I've grown up within Judaism, but I didn't really appreciate this fully until I went to Israel in 2006. While I was there on a teen mission to the country, the Israel-Hezbollah war started and rockets came into northern Israel. We were visiting a *kibbutz* in that region when an explosion went off not far from us. We felt the vibration. I could hear people screaming, and first they had us gather in a cafeteria—then, they had us all get into a bomb shelter.

This was so scary that I thought: We are going to die.

But then I began to think: No, my ancestors are all around me, here in this land. I envisioned them around me like you might think of angels hovering around. Then, I knew we'd be safe. And we were.

I did have to leave the country early with my group because of the war, but this made a life-changing impression on me. Israel is the land of our heritage, and our hope of a peaceful trip to this homeland had ended in violence—in war.

At my school, when I got back home, I thought that we should start a diversity club. I wanted to bring people together and work toward peace in the world. I wanted more than handshakes. I wanted our relationships to mean something.

People are so segregated in the way they live their daily lives today; often, people are not even trying to meet or understand different people.

My idea for an organization at school started in a small way. At first, the vice principal didn't seem at all supportive of having a diversity club. As students, we said to one another: What do we do now? Our vice principal doesn't even want to help start something like this. Can we do it? We could see that this was going to be a long process. We had to figure out the next steps on our own.

So, the group began to meet. My brother—we're twins—was part of it and helped, too. We all got together at someone's house and we began to discuss what this group might do together. Even by participating in those meetings, we opened ourselves up to others. I'm Jewish, and some of my Jewish friends were part of this, but we stopped being just a group of Jewish friends. Now, we were talking together as Jews, Muslims, Christians and others, too. We brought in Brenda Rosenberg from WISDOM to help us. We started planning for speakers who would come into the school from different cultures and religious groups. We planned for a Muslim speaker and our first speaker in the schedule was a rabbi.

This wasn't easy. We faced problems. When the rabbi came to speak, one of the teachers started freaking out about things the rabbi was saying. Her emotional response then offended some of the Jewish students in the audience. Then, we were afraid to bring in our next speaker, the Muslim, because we feared the reactions we might get. We had hoped to proudly show off these speakers—really welcome them to our school, and have them share their wisdom with us. Instead, it was an uncomfortable experience—largely because of responses we got from the school staff.

The students were more open. My best friend is Catholic, for example, and she found the rabbi's talk very interesting.

We kept working at it. We kept meeting and we kept planning. We started out with maybe 10 or 12 people, and now I think there are 25 or 30 people. I moved on to college, but my younger sister is still in the school and now is the president of the diversity club.

Now that I've moved on to college, I realize that what we started was very important. I'm a sophomore now at the university and I realize that, at this age, we're already moving out into a much larger world. There are fewer people trying to arrange things in our lives, encouraging us to fit into particular groups. Now, it's our choice who we'll talk with, where we'll go and what friendships we'll form. Many people choose to stay within a little bubble of people who are just like them. But I've learned how important it is to reach out beyond that comfortable bubble. That's our hope for a better world.

Patty's Story:

I've always tried to help out when parents were needed at school. Elana went to a Jewish school for some years, but then she went into a public school, so she—and I—had both kinds of experiences.

My family placed emphasis on the importance of simply trying to do the right thing each and every day. I grew up with a very strong commitment to being a fair person, an honest person—a person who would always stand up for what is right over what is wrong. I taught that to my own children.

The biggest question I've had about religion through the years is this: Religion is supposed to create harmony—so why does it often do the opposite? Originally, religion was supposed to unify people: to bring them together in communities and to establish rules that would guide people in fair and peaceful ways. But as religions developed over so many centuries, it seems as though religion now separates people more than it unites them. You can see the segregation in so many places. In a high school, just look at who sits together in the lunchroom: You'll see the separation right there.

So, when my daughter Elana wanted to start this diversity club—and her brother agreed to help her—I thought it was a good idea. There was a lot of thinking behind Elana's idea. She had been in Israel. She also had read *The Kite Runner,* and she saw in that book how people could be discriminated against even within their own religious group. She felt very strongly that she should start doing something about these problems.

I wanted to help my kids get the Diversity Club off the ground. But it's difficult for parents, too. You have to be careful and balance your own involvement.

This did take a whole lot of effort from the kids themselves. At first, many of the kids in the club were Jewish. They invited others to join the group, but it took time to grow and make new friends. Over time, it did open up and more kids got involved.

As a parent, I teach my children that the goal in life is to become a good person who helps other people. That's not the main message our culture sends to young people today. Have you watched TV shows like *Survivor*? There are so many messages on TV and in other media saying that life is all about competition—beat the other guy and win at all costs. As parents, we've got to show kids that there's an alternative to that kind of competition.

You can call me Suzie Sunshine for talking like this. I've gotten burned plenty of times because of my outlook on life, but I remain optimistic. I still believe it's important to encourage hope and cooperation among people. Sometimes, people aren't ready for that. But I keep working at it, because most people really are good—you just have to give them a chance to do the right thing.

I'm not naïve. I know what goes on, even among good kids—problems like cyber-bullying can become very painful. I've seen this firsthand, and I tell other parents that we have to be involved in our kids' lives.

So, as other parents read our story, I hope they will feel inspired to become active and to try ideas like a diversity club. Remember that it won't be easy.

But you know what? All you can do is wake up each morning and try to do the right thing.

Elana's Final Word:

Now that I'm in college, I realize how important it has been for me to meet older women through groups like WIS-DOM. Women in WISDOM helped me even while I was in high school, working on our diversity club. Now, I realize how much I can learn from these women.

Just seeing them together, talking and working on things, is inspiring. When I see that—these women with so many differences in their lives working together—I realize that it is possible for adults to work together as friends. It is possible to stop focusing on things like the clothes each person wears or his or her religious background—and to focus instead on people's hearts. For me, it's a wonderful experience just to walk into a room and spend time with women like this.

CHAPTER 22

Brenda Naomi Rosenberg

The Courage to Follow a Vision Toward Peace

Sometimes tiny sparks trigger bombs; sometimes they light candles.

Brenda is active in her Jewish congregation and in Jewish causes around the world. Her earlier career in fashion marketing gave her decades of experience in moving confidently across geographic and cultural boundaries. Here is her story of an idea—rooted in friendship—that is making a difference around the world.

I grew up around bright lights. My parents owned the Raven Gallery in Detroit, a meeting place for artists, musicians, writers and civic activists. In my 20s I began a long career in fashion marketing, and eventually was named Vice President of Fashion Merchandising and Marketing for Federated and Allied Department Stores. At the chain's height, I identified the trends that would show up in more than 1,000 stores—including Hudson's in Michigan, Bloomingdale's in New York, Burdines in Florida and Bullock's in California. I've traveled widely, rubbing shoulders with the rich and famous—I even dined in Monaco with Prince Rainier III—and to this day, I have friends from nearly every cultural background you can imagine.

But, my work over the last decade has taken more courage than anything I experienced in my business career. As a Jewish woman who cares about her Jewish community and about Israel, it was a controversial decision to devote my life after September 11, 2001, to bringing Christians, Muslims and Jews together.

It has not gotten any easier over the years! After the war between Israel and Hezbollah, keeping friendships on both sides of the divide took daring, stubborn determination and a clear vision that our hope for peace depends on maintaining all relationships. But that is where peace begins—in the relationships we form as we break bread together, share our stories with each other and begin to work together. That's when the light begins to shine.

We have to look closely for those first flashes of light. Sometimes tiny sparks trigger bombs; sometimes they light candles.

One of those sparks flashed in my life after a lunch with my friend Imam Abdullah El-Amin, who is assistant imam at Detroit's largest Muslim center. We are unlikely friends: He's a 6-foot-6-inch, male, African-American, Muslim leader and I'm a 5-foot-3-inch, female, Jewish peace activist; he's based in the heart of Detroit and I'm based in the suburbs. After an interfaith luncheon in the spring of 2003, we walked to our cars and continued to talk about all of the problems in the world that involve Jews, Christians and Muslims. "If we would only remember that we all share the same father, Abraham," Abdullah said to me, "then we might find ways to bring our family back together again." He reminded me of a passage in the Bible in which Abraham's two sons—Ishmael and Isaac—had been separated for many years. In spite of that, they came together at Abraham's death to bury their father. Then, Abdullah said to me: "We're tearing our world apart today. Why can't we do what Ishmael and Isaac did, and come back together as a family?"

All that day, I thought about his words. I couldn't stop thinking about Ishmael and Isaac reuniting, after all the hurt and anger they felt toward each other.

That night, I had a dream about a stage in a theater. On it, I saw Isaac and Ishmael leaving the caves of Machpelah—the burial site of Abraham—together. As they started to turn away from each other, the Archangel Raphaella flew in from stage left and wrapped her wings around the grieving brothers, asking them to sit down. She guided them through a four-step healing process.

The following week I met with Abdullah and another friend, the Rev. Dan Buttry, who is head of global reconciliation for American Baptist Churches. We felt that my dream could evolve into a new kind of peace initiative that would give us the opportunity to bring our fragmented communities together. We could tell the story of Abraham and his two sons, Isaac and Ishmael, in a new light. We could take the 2,000-year-old sibling rivalry, the brothers' posturing for a father's love, the demands for a fair share of the inheritance—both in terms of land and ideology—and retell the story to help people heal the trans-generational wounds that have imprisoned us in a cycle of fear, hate and intolerance. The idea for "Reuniting the Children of Abraham" was born.

Our next step was to find Metro Detroit teenagers from all three faiths willing to share personal stories about their experiences with the boundaries of faith and ethnicity. We were shocked to hear that every teen had been subjected to some form of religious, cultural or racial prejudice. Many already had developed a real fear of the "other." We used the four-step process of reconciliation with these teens: Step 1, breaking bread together, which turned into sharing pizza; step 2, sharing our deeply personal stories with the group, including ways in which we have been hurt; step 3, having someone else retell our stories; and step 4, collaborating on a project, which became "Reuniting the Children of Abraham." From the beginning, it was far more than a theatrical production. We extended the experience into sessions during which the audience could talk with the young actors and with one another about the ideas we were presenting. We saw we had the potential to help communities not only in Michigan, but across the country and around the world.

That expansion took a whole lot of friends! Victor Begg, co-chair of the Council of Islamic Organizations of Michigan, encouraged two of his children, Sofia Begg Latif and Yousuf Begg, to take part in the original workshop. My friend Julie Cummings was supportive from the beginning, and her family and my family were among five—Cummings, Seligman, Farbman, Gershenson and Rosenberg—that donated funds to produce "Reuniting the Children of Abraham." Entire cities got involved. The Kalamazoo-based Fetzer Institute both funded and brought a production to Kalamazoo and worked hard to bring many different groups together in its region of southwest Michigan.

Media professionals joined our ever-widening circle. The CBS television network produced a documentary about the project that aired nationwide, and we were featured in an hour-long special on Bridges TV, a national Muslim television network.

"Reuniting the Children of Abraham" now has friends all around the world. In 2006, we were asked to speak to more than 400 psychologists and psychotherapists from 70 countries at the New Ways of Looking at Conflict Conference in Israel. While there, we also met with Arab and Israeli high school students who participate in a similar project called "Peace Child Israel." They were shocked to learn that the Middle East conflict affects high school students in the U.S.

The project has opened many doors. Imam Elahi gave me the honor of being the first Jewish woman to deliver a Ramadan sermon at a mosque in Michigan. Imam Abdullah El-Amin and I were keynote speakers at the 2006 National Humanities Conference in Louisville, Kentucky. In Atlanta, we spoke to more than 300 Jewish educators, most of whom had never met an imam. In 2007, I orchestrated an invitation for Victor Begg to address a national conference of rabbis—and Victor arranged for me to present "Reuniting the Children of Abraham" at the Islamic Society of North America, a gathering of thousands of Muslims. In 2008, we were guests of the royal family in Amman, Jordan, where we presented the documentary in Arabic. That Arabic translation was a gift of another friend, Mona Farouk, whose story also appears in this book.

The project since 2005 has been packaged as a multimedia tool kit for peace, complete with a CD of educational material and a 40-minute documentary on DVD. That's all part of the ongoing Web site: www.TheChildrenofAbraham-Project.org. Through all of this work and all of these travels, what interests me most is the question that started me on this long journey: Where can we find those individual sparks of light? I'm always looking for the change we can make in each life and each new friendship.

In 2004, our project became part of the first Midwest Palestinian-Jewish Dialogue Weekend (organized by more good friends, Len and Libby Traubman), held in Duluth, Minnesota.

At this dialogue weekend, we gathered in a circle to tell our stories. There was a young Muslim Palestinian woman who had arrived for the weekend with a very skeptical view of what we might achieve together. She retold her story of growing up in a refugee camp. She spoke of hardships and she shared how terrified she was of Israeli soldiers. She had witnessed a soldier shooting a child in the arms of a mother. At one point, she burst into tears and said she hated Jews.

She left the group and nearly left the entire program. I encouraged her to remain—and she did. As we had listened to her stories in our circle, she now took the time to hear Jewish stories. She learned about the Holocaust for the first time from a survivor. We shared a great deal more in the next two days, but most importantly, we shared our desire to work toward peace. This young woman sat next to me as we watched a presentation of "Reuniting the Children of Abraham." We cried together for the past, but we also shed tears of hope for what the future might hold. After the presentation she asked for the microphone and said: "When I arrived on Friday, I hated Jews. I thought this weekend was going to be a waste of time. But now I know Palestinians and Jews can talk. I know now that peace is possible, and I can even call a Jew my friend"—and she gave me a hug in front of 600 people.

That's what renews my courage. That's the kind of miraculous spark I keep searching for wherever I travel around the world. That's the pathway of friendship that leads to peace.

CHAPTER 23

Gail Katz

A Journey Outward—and Inward

How can I describe the pleasure that I get watching the faces of 150 seventh-graders, their parents and their teachers, as we come together with rabbis, imams, priests and other clergy?

Gail is an educator whose talents have led her to help found—or to dramatically reshape—various community groups, programs and activities over the years. In her story, she explores the roots of that creative activism. She also explains how this daring embrace of diversity has deepened the core of her own faith.

As an interfaith activist, I'm often asked where my ideas and my energy for this work originated. To trace my long journey toward the creative ideas that now define my life, I have to travel back to my years growing up in a post-war, secular, Jewish family. You may not be Jewish yourself, but you may find yourself connecting with such early memories. Throughout my life, I've met many adults whose attitudes toward diversity were shaped when they were very young. I spent my early childhood and my elementary school years in Silver Spring, Maryland, in a rather non-Jewish neighborhood. I was one of a few Jewish children in my school. The memories that have stuck with me are ones of feeling different from my neighbors and my classmates. I started each morning bowing my head with all the other children and saying the Lord's Prayer in my public school classroom, and even in my sleep today I can recite "Our Father, who art in Heaven, hallowed be thy name ..." But I knew, deep inside me, that this was really not my prayer. At Christmastime, we had Christmas plays and sang songs like *Silent Night, Oh Come All Ye Faithful* and *Joy to the World*. Although I sang along, I knew that these were not my songs.

Every year I had to bring in my family menorah and explain the meaning of Hanukkah. For an extremely shy child, this was absolute torture—singled out in front of the class as different. I begged my mother to buy us Glass Wax, made by Gold Seal, so that my brother and I could participate in the same traditions as my classmates and make snowflake stencils on the windows, since we were not allowed to put up a Christmas tree.

My Judaism mostly revolved around holidays. We would go to the synagogue on Rosh Hashanah and Yom Kippur, and we had the family over for Passover and Hanukkah. I had no idea about other Jewish holidays, and when I was taken to our synagogue in Montgomery County, Maryland, my memories were again about feeling different and uncomfortable. My family only sent my brother to Hebrew School to prepare for his bar mitzvah. Girls were not expected, in the 1950s, to get any real Jewish education. So, as a child, I felt conspicuous for not knowing how to read or recite the Hebrew prayers. I would sit next to my father, playing with the *tsitsit* (the fringes) on his *tallit* (prayer shawl), waiting impatiently to go home. There was always this sense of anger inside me that I didn't fit in at school or in my Jewish community.

When I was 12 years old, my father got a job with Ford Motor Company and we moved to Oak Park, a suburb of Detroit. In 1960, Oak Park had a sizable Jewish population, and my junior high school was about 85 percent Jewish. My junior high school years were difficult ones for me: I still felt different, even though I was now in classes with many Jewish students. I was a target for bullying as the "new kid," the "quiet kid" and the "all-A" student. My sense of outrage at not being given respect for being different from the "cool" kids laid the foundation for my later passion in helping students organize diversity clubs.

While all of this was unfolding, my mother's father came from Far Rockaway, NY, to live with us. My Grandpa Aron was very religious, spoke mostly Yiddish, and reminisced with my mother about the old country. His world was the old Russia, which was taken over by Poland by the time my mother was born, and is today part of Belarus. I loved him dearly. Although we had a hard time communicating with words, we did just fine with kisses and embraces, and I have to admit that I picked up quite a bit of Yiddish along the way.

I learned from my grandfather about his world of Eastern European Jewry, his love for the Torah, his need to keep kosher, his *davening* (praying) and his Jewish custom of putting on *tefillin* (phylacteries) every morning in his bedroom. Our Passover Seders became very traditional, and to this day we sing out my grandfather's Eastern European Jewish prayers from the Haggadah (Passover prayer book) every year. I grew up with Holocaust stories—my mother's cousins, aunts and uncles had perished in the concentration camps—and I knew that my mother was alive only because my grandfather had the foresight to get his family out of Poland in the late 1920s.

My mother and father made their children keenly aware of our calling as Jews to *Tikkun Olam* (repairing the world). There were Russian Jewish immigrants at our Passover Seders every year. My mother and I marched together in Washington, DC to highlight the urgency of bringing persecuted Jews from the former USSR to the United States. During my senior year in high school, my family housed a foreign exchange student from Brazil and we talked often about championing the rights of African-Americans in the South.

Because of my grandfather's and my mother's immigrant family background, I was drawn toward a career of teaching English to immigrants. From the time I graduated college, I spent my time teaching English as a Second Language to adults, and then finally teaching children in public schools. I saw how these students felt ostracized because of their struggle with the English language, their different cultures and religions, and their different economic status.

I formed a diversity club called STARS (Students Taking a Right Stand) to help address these problems, among others. We addressed all of our differences, celebrated our diversity, and learned how to stand up and speak out against bullying. We ran Family Heritage Fairs, displayed portraits of Holocaust survivors, sponsored No Name Calling Week and Mix-It-Up at Lunch Day, and put together an Ellis Island simulation for the entire school, to highlight everyone's cultural heritage.

It was during my teaching career in the Berkley School District that I noticed an article in the *Jewish News* about a grant that the Jewish Community Relations Council received to sponsor a Religious Diversity Initiative. It didn't take long for me to get on the committee, then chair the committee, and finally become the coordinator of the program entitled the Religious Diversity Journeys for Seventh Graders, which is now run by the Michigan Roundtable for Diversity and Inclusion. This wonderful program for seventh-graders in six school districts in Oakland County, just north of Detroit, promotes greater awareness and understanding of the many religions prevalent in metro Detroit and prepares students for life in our increasingly diverse society.

In the program, 25 students from each of the six school districts participate in five school-day field trips between January and May to focus on the differences and similarities among some of the major religions found in our community, including Christianity, Judaism, Islam, Hinduism, Buddhism and Sikhism. We visit a different array of temples and other houses of worship each year.

How can I describe the pleasure that I get watching the faces of 150 seventh-graders, their parents and their teachers as we come together with rabbis, imams, priests and other clergy to expand our horizons as a community?

A big step along my own journey was the nationally-known World Views Seminar at the University of Michigan-Dearborn. Each year, men and women from across the country enroll in this intensive, short-term program that immerses people in a wide range of religious traditions, including visits to many houses of worship. This academic program further fueled my passion to promote diversity, and I was drawn toward another widely-known program: the annual World Sabbath for Religious Reconciliation, held each January at Christ Church Cranbrook, a historic landmark here in Michigan. I got so involved that I wound up as chairperson of the planning committee.

Before I got involved, the World Sabbath focused on prayers for world peace by the clergy of different religious institutions, but we shifted our focus toward youth—letting them actually lead the rest of us in prayers for peace, entertaining us with dance and music and creating peace banners that are woven into a Children of Peace Quilt.

In March of 2006, I met my spiritual soul mates: Trish, a Christian, and Shahina, a Muslim, at Brenda Rosenberg's "Reuniting the Children of Abraham," a unique interfaith experience about connections between Judaism, Christianity and Islam. With my soul mates, I became one of the co-founders of WISDOM—Women's Interfaith Solutions for Dialogue and Outreach in MetroDetroit—a story you'll read at the beginning of this book.

What's most remarkable about my journey is that it has not led me away from my own faith! On the contrary, my quest has strengthened and deepened my Judaism.

In championing and celebrating "the other," I have reconnected with my own childhood yearning. I have come full circle—from the days of feeling "left out" as a youngster, to conquering that feeling by enrolling as an adult in a Torah study class and attending Jewish retreats. I am awed by this turn in my long quest—taking me home even as it has carried me so far from my home.

My journey continues—outward and inward. Wherever you live as you are reading this, think about starting a journey of your own. You're likely to find your own tradition enriched even as you reach out to explore the larger world with others.

Part VI

A Lifetime of Wider Vision

CHAPTER 24

Elaine M. Schonberger

Handing Down an Awareness of Community

*It opened their eyes, just as
we had hoped*

Elaine is an educator and
a community activist who
often volunteers her time
to promote diversity and
human rights. She is able to
look across nearly a century
of her own Jewish family's
life in the U.S.—and see
a legacy of cross-cultural
relationships.

Interfaith relationships have been around for a long time in America; they have been a part of my family since before I was born, in the 1950s. They are the means by which my parents related to their community, whatever the religion or race or ethnicity of our neighbors was. As children, we were taught to be extremely respectful of other people and to help anyone who needed our help—this was the lesson in our home from day one.

My father, Izzy Malin, devoted his life to these relationships. He was a businessman—a salesman in the wholesale food business—and he understood that everyone should pitch in to help the community. As we were growing up in northwest Detroit, I remember my parents volunteering in community efforts at local Catholic parishes as well as in the Jewish community. Over the years, my parents were honored by Catholic leaders for their efforts. My father had Arab-American friends, some of whom were Christian and others Muslim. He met them through the grocery business, and he was known for helping these friends get their grocery stores started, in many cases.

In 1982, my father and my mother, Frances, helped to found the American Arab and Jewish Friends. Today, we're seeing new approaches to diversity in groups like WISDOM, but the Friends group my parents co-founded was very important for many years. Their group brought together a lot of business people and community leaders to do good things together.

My husband and I lived in Texas in the 1980s, but when we moved back to Michigan in 1990, I saw more of the work they were doing firsthand. I got involved in similar efforts myself, working on projects like United We Walk, which was an annual Martin Luther King Day observance. I was also the only parent on a multicultural committee in local schools; the other members of the committee were educators and staff members.

One good idea my parents helped to get started through the Friends group was an essay contest for high-school students. The contest was quite involved: Each year, the Friends group sent out packets to local schools, inviting students to apply for this scholarship competition. Then, the Friends group would help interested students organize themselves into groups of three—usually including a Christian, a Muslim and a Jew. The three would have to complete a number of activities together over several months: They had to visit each of the three homes, and experience a meal of foods that were typically a part of each cultural group; they would visit one other's place of worship, too. Then they would prepare their final essays. Each student had to write an essay about his or her personal experience—and then they would write a fourth essay, "The Ties That Bind," with input from all three students. We usually got 25 or 30 of these completed packets each year.

I always knew that the scholarship competition was an important program and, after my father died in 1999, I volunteered to help lead the Friends group and coordinate the essay contest for a while. The group no longer exists, but in the year 2000, I had a chance to see what a big impact the essay contest had on my own family.

My son Michael was a senior, and he wanted to complete the "The Ties That Bind" project. He found two other students to join him: One was a Muslim and one was an Iraqi-American Christian.

I still remember the night they came to our home. My mother visited just to be a part of it that night. This was a program she and my father had started years before, and her grandson, Michael, was going through it now with other students. I fixed chicken soup with matzo balls, a brisket and some other traditional dishes. I served them gefilte fish. My mother and I were thrilled to see this.

In the final essays, each student talked about what he learned, but what impressed me was the way they all found similarities between our cultures. Even in our places of worship, they realized that many of the prayers and blessings were similar. It opened their eyes just as we had hoped.

I was born into interfaith work. This was just a part of life in my family. My parents always understood that a healthy community depends on various faiths, races and cultures all working together. They saw this, partly because they were in business and they understood the networks that can make this country a better place for everyone. And I thank God now that they had those insights. They didn't teach me tolerance—that was not enough. They taught their children acceptance and appreciation and the importance of joining hands to work together.

Unfortunately, the world has changed in many ways. The Friends group doesn't exist anymore. The scholarship program ended, although I think the idea is still a good one. These days, fewer people have the time—or take the time—to work on this kind of outreach that we once saw as so vital.

But I certainly hope that the larger legacy I inherited—passed along to my sons Michael and Keith—is not over. I know my sons now are involved in groups that promote these same goals. My husband, Mark, and I are very proud of them. My parents would be as well. We need to keep forming strong relationships like this in each new generation. The work needs to continue.

CHAPTER 25

Ellen Ehrlich
Freeing Friends from Boxes

In accepting all people, our community becomes a reflection of the real world.

Like millions of Americans, Ellen has moved through a wide range of religious experiences in her life. Born into a New York Jewish family, she moved through Christian Fundamentalism, home churches and even a period of secular inactivity. Today, she's active in a diverse Episcopal Church in Royal Oak, a city north of Detroit. Similarly, Ellen's professional career has ranged widely from years as an American media executive in print publications and network TV news—to her current work as a Realtor. Her breadth of experience has led her to deeply appreciate the rare value of nonjudgmental acceptance in friendship.

"**W**hat are you?"

When someone asks me that question about my religious affiliation, I remember something a friend told me back while I was involved in a house church in New York. That day I was very upset about something that had happened, and my friend Bob told me: "Never let anybody put you into a box."

I have tried to live my life that way—by not putting myself into a box and not putting anyone else into a box. The problem is that as soon as we're stuck in a mental box, or we put other people in a box—whether it's a professional, theological, spiritual, sexual or political box—then that's how you're defined in another person's mind. And you're never going to get back out of that box, in most cases. You're stuck.

If you do that to other people, then it's hard to be fully accepting.

I was born Jewish. Now, I say I'm an Episcopalian. I don't say I'm "Christian"—that word describes a particular box for most people. Sometimes I do have fun with these ways of defining myself. In church, I remember someone saying that, spiritually speaking, "We're all 'adopted.'"

I said, "No, you might be 'adopted.' I was chosen!"

It's important to be aware of these boxes, because there are a lot of people eager to push others into them for their own purposes. Back in the 1980s, when I was working for NBC News, I went back and forth to Los Angeles each year. Once, a friend invited me to visit a church on Wilshire Boulevard in Beverly Hills. It turned out to be this nondenominational church with a rock band on stage and, soon, people around me were speaking in tongues. At that point I was sliding down in my chair, trying to be invisible, because I didn't want to be around these people. But the whole thing works on you. At the end, the minister on stage asked, "Does anybody here want to accept Jesus Christ as their Lord and

Savior?" And, my hand went up! I always want to deny that I actually raised my hand, but it happened. My hand went up! The next thing I knew, I was taken someplace where people were praying and talking to us about starting Bible studies and I was already saying to myself: It's going to be OK. I'm going back to New York soon. It's going to be OK.

My church now, St. John's Episcopal, is the perfect church for me. Here, everyone is accepted. Everyone is welcome. We have a sign that says "You are welcome" and at this church, we mean it. There are people who drive long distances to attend this church.

In accepting all people, our community becomes a reflection of the real world. We have people here who are barely subsisting on Social Security and also one of the top executives in an auto company. We have people with a high school education and people who have earned doctorates. We have white and black, straight and gay and people with ethnicities from around the world. Of course, God accepts all of us no matter who or where we are—but there are not enough institutions of faith out there with God's level of acceptance.

I became involved in the WISDOM interfaith group of women to have another circle of friends beyond my church and my work as a Realtor. I appreciate that, in this group, people do not try to convert one another. They take acceptance seriously, too.

I'm on the WISDOM board, and my Hindu friend doesn't try to convert me. Our Muslim friend doesn't say to our Hindu friend, "How can you be Hindu? Why don't you consider converting?" None of us evangelizes anyone else.

This behavior allows us to really learn about each other and, after many years working in network news, I can tell you: Americans need to know a whole lot more about the world. I still read *The New York Times* every day, but the American public's awareness of the larger world is shrinking so fast that many people now think the world can fit into a YouTube screen and a few 140-character Tweets. That lack of awareness is what leads people to slip back into an "Us vs. Them" view of the world. People become polarized. Right now, there are strong signs that we are moving away from acceptance. All of these angry, random sound bytes surrounding us these days are pushing people toward the extremes. The middle ground of acceptance is vanishing. We all need to work on restoring it.

That's why I appreciate so much the circles of friends in my church and in WISDOM who understand the importance of acceptance.

The only box that's healthy is a box so big that it can hold all of us without anyone ever bumping into a wall.

CHAPTER 26

Anjali Vale

Seeking Common Wavelengths

I believe that every human is the manifestation of God, and I bow to that divinity.

Anjali came to the U.S. with her new husband when she was young. Now the parents of two teenage boys, she and her husband are comfortably adapted to life in America. A working mother and practicing Hindu, Anjali describes how her own deep appreciation for the world's diversity grew throughout her life—and she offers hope that the world is, indeed, catching on to this important idea.

I moved to the United States from India many years ago with my new husband. We married soon after we first met, and so all at once I had a new land to make my home, a new husband to make my family, and new people to make my friends. Although I was scared and anxious, I was hopeful that, with some work, I would enjoy my new home, family and friends.

Both of my parents, by their behavior, had taught me to have an open mind, to not judge people and to help wherever there is need. They never forced my brother or me to do things or make decisions based on their views, but instead gave us the freedom to choose. My parents always believed in us – believed that we would do the right thing. Their faith in us meant a lot to me.

I always saw my mother, who is a doctor, helping others—even in the middle of the night if someone came knocking on the door with a pain or wound. I saw her travel extra distances to visit and support patients or friends. My dad is a great philosopher who does a great deal of reading of Indian literature. Now that I am a parent raising my own family and have experienced the world a bit, I feel even closer to my parents, and I appreciate and understand them even more.

Growing up in India, I never felt that faith separated people. India is a diverse country with various languages, castes, and religions. I am Hindu, but my very good friends who helped me grow were of different faiths. After coming to the U.S., I feel strongly that, if your wavelengths match, you can build a strong relationship with any human being, no matter the religion, gender or age of that person.

After finishing my Master of Science in the U.S., I began working as an instructor; it was my first job in my new environment. I still remember that time: My son was just a year old, I had a new job, and I had no family nearby to rely on.

It was a time full of anxiety. At work, a colleague who was older and more experienced helped me through that difficult time. Most of my support was coming from a person who was American and of a different race, faith, and nationality. But I don't think we even talked about faith then. She gave me the sense of belonging that I needed. Similarly, a few other new friends from various backgrounds made me feel at home here.

Raising my children in the States has required me to find a balance in mixing our Indian culture and Hindu faith with our life in America. I teach my sons the pieces that are most important and that they can adapt themselves as Indian-Americans. I hope that, as adults, they will have the best values from both societies.

When I go back to India, to my hometown outside Mumbai, people say, "You are different than before. The U.S. has changed you." I suppose they are right. But I also see a change in the people of India. Life there used to be slow and informal. When I was young, my mother would run an errand and be out for hours, talking to people she ran into along the way. Today, however, people are often in a hurry. Along with a faster pace, people seem to have adopted a more open attitude to the rest of the world. Along with me, India has changed.

Now I have all types of friends from work and the local community, including friends from Ukraine and Japan. We converse about various topics such as the stock market, philosophy or yoga. In India, many faiths coexist peacefully, and I grew up with friends of both genders and of different languages and ethnic backgrounds. I believe every human being is basically the same.

If you have respect and understanding for others, then people will reciprocate the same respect and understanding. People may have different opinions, but if you talk things out with an open mind and try to understand what the other person is thinking, friendship develops. But if people start making assumptions, and no one is paying attention to what the other is thinking, it is very easy to misunderstand each other and lose a friendship over simple things.

Growing up, I was taught the basic values of Hinduism such as respect for other souls, tolerance and pluralism, which for me means that I see all religious paths as equally valid. I am a firm believer that my path is not the only one toward the Supreme God or divinity, but that there may be many true and meaningful paths.

The experiences in my life, with all the people I've met, have taught me to respect other people's races, faiths, nationalities and, most importantly, to simply respect others as human beings. Our outside appearances differ, but, inside, every human being is one and the same.

I believe that every human is the manifestation of God, and I bow to that divinity.

Namaste!

CHAPTER 27

Fran Shiovitz Hildebrandt

Crossing Boundaries in Marriage

When you're talking about your spiritual self, how can you ask someone to compromise?

Fran is a practicing conservative Jew who has honored her interfaith marriage for 35 years. Fran grew up surrounded by neighbors who practiced tolerance and acceptance, despite their cultural and religious  differences. That welcoming community, followed by her experience living overseas—and her husband's support of her religious beliefs—have all made Fran who she is today.

As a child, I had the same kinds of experiences as many non-Christian kids in that era, when schools were not as diverse as they are today. We were expected to participate in Christian holiday activities, such as singing Christmas carols or making Easter eggs. Certainly I recognized that my own religion was being ignored.

But in my neighborhood, there was tolerance and acceptance. Families were friends based on interests and activities. As children, we played with everyone. No distinctions were made by religion. Our parents helped one another, and our friendships were based on our similarities. I saw it as an ideal community. Looking back, I realize that I was given the opportunity to view the world through unbiased eyes—to see people in a positive way.

At the same time, my parents were instilling in my brothers, sister and me a strong sense of identity as Jews and a strong foundation in Judaism.

I was brought up in a conservative Jewish home. My parents kept kosher and observed the holidays. They were active in our synagogue. We attended religious school and synagogue services. But as I got older, I was encouraged to socialize primarily with other Jewish kids. That continued until college, where I met friends who were not Jewish, some of whom are still close friends today. I also met my husband in college.

Certainly my parents would have preferred that I marry someone Jewish, but as it turned out, my parents loved my husband! We connected with each other based on our similarities, and not our differences. Yet, because of my husband's beliefs, he did not feel slighted or disrespected by my faith. We waited six years to get married, until we worked everything out, although I don't think we'll ever work out all of the quirks.

It's hard to combine faiths on a daily basis. We maintain a Jewish home in which we keep kosher and observe the holidays. (Our friends and family are both amused and amazed at how well my husband can conduct a seder.) I am active in my synagogue. My husband attends services and synagogue functions with me. He maintains his own beliefs but is able to integrate them with my practice of Judaism. We have tried to have a marriage that is based on love and mutual respect for each other's beliefs. I give my husband a lot of credit, because he has had to make more compromises than I have.

According to Jewish law, a child born of a Jewish woman or a convert to Judaism is Jewish. At the beginning of our marriage, we agreed that our children would be raised Jewishly. We would actively help each of them to develop a strong Jewish identity that would be religious, cultural, and social. We kept this promise.

Since we did not have a Christmas tree in our home, our family spent Christmas with my husband's parents. The boys understood that Christmas was not their holiday—that it was Grandpa's and Grandma's holiday—but they were allowed to enjoy it, as Jews, and not feel guilty. Easter often falls right during Passover, so we handled it differently as the boys got older. Sometimes I would bring kosher for Passover food with me to serve at my husband's parents' home. Other times they came to our home on Passover and I would serve a kosher for Passover Easter dinner. Both sets of grandparents were friendly toward each other, so we were able to spend birthdays and Mother's Day and Father's Day together.

I'm not a proponent of mixed marriages. At its best, marriage is difficult. There are always problems and conflicts, and based on today's statistics, not many people seem willing or able to resolve the tough issues couples face. When the partners in a marriage practice two different religions, life is even more complicated. When you're talking about your spiritual self, how can you ask someone to compromise?

For those considering an interfaith marriage, I would recommend you do the following: Attend services of the other person's faith and participate in family holidays—see if each of you can feel comfortable doing this. I also recommend taking a class that presents an objective point of view of the religion of your partner. It's another opportunity to learn if you could be comfortable being part of someone else's faith. And finally, talk to couples (as in more than one) in interfaith marriages. Learn firsthand some of the joys and pitfalls that a mixed marriage creates.

Having an interfaith marriage has given my sons a different perspective on spirituality and diversity. They have much more respect and appreciation for various spiritual and cultural traditions. My sons have had opportunities to see religion function at its best and also the way it can create suspicion and separation. Our family experiences have taught them the importance of communication combined with love and respect.

Living overseas also shaped who I am today. My husband and I, along with our two oldest sons, lived in Medan, N. Sumatra, Indonesia for two years. We lived and taught in a Muslim community. This was an amazing chance to experience other cultures and, as a Jew, it was especially gratifying to feel accepted by such a diverse religious community as existed in Medan. Today I teach high school English in a very non-Jewish community; I don't know if I could do this so successfully without the childhood and life experiences I've had. My husband is a remarkable man who has taught me a lot. Even after all these years, there are still new questions about Judaism that arise. When that happens, it is often because my husband will ask why I want to do something. Sometimes I have to re-learn it to explain it. More importantly, it forces me to analyze, "Why *do* I do this? Why *is* this important to me?" Sometimes I have taken rituals for granted.

One of the benefits of having a husband like mine is having a partner who respects and honors Judaism. The more I'm around people who are not Jewish, the more it makes me appreciate my own religion. We've been married for 35 years—together for 41 years—and my husband has really helped to make me a better Jew.

CHAPTER 28

Shahina Begg
Reaching Out, Generation to Generation

As I set off on this long journey, I had no idea how the meeting with Victor's parents would go.

Shahina is a co-founder of WISDOM, so she also is part of this book's opening chapter. Within her own family, Shahina is part of a remarkable multi-generational tradition of crossing boundaries in friendship. Born and raised in Hinduism, she converted to Islam as an adult. After reading Shahina's story here, you will meet Shahina's daughter in the next chapter.

This is the story of how I first met one of my best friends in life—and it was not at all what I expected when I set out on this long journey.

I was born into a Brahmin-class family in Hinduism. Of course, the caste system is not as important as it once was, but our culture and our Hindu traditions were important to my family. We did not go to the temple frequently, but we always visited the temple for special occasions. To this day, when my siblings visit my mother near Goa, in western India, she takes them to the temple. Because I converted to Islam, I no longer go to the temple like they do—but I always make sure that my mother is able to visit a temple here in the U.S., when she comes to see us.

My own interfaith journey began in my childhood and has extended through my entire life. I grew up in Bombay, now Mumbai, which is a very cosmopolitan city; I had friends of different faiths as I was growing up. Dad was the assistant commissioner of police for Bombay and Mom was a homemaker.

I came to America in 1973 and began working on a Master's in Business Administration in January of 1974. That's when I first met my husband, Victor, who was studying business as well. I was 20 and Victor was a little older. About a year and a half later, we got married. When I first came to America, I wasn't sure if I was going to stay here for good—but meeting Victor made the difference.

My dad was very open-minded when he heard the news. At first—as many Indian families do—he wanted to check on Victor's family. He was very busy with his police work at the time, so at first he sent one of his officers over from Bombay to Hyderabad, where Victor's family lived. However, this officer came back and said: "There's some problem with the family address. I can't find the place."

Dad asked me about this, and I said, "There must be some mistake."

Finally, my father himself went to Hyderabad. He met Victor's family and he said to me, "Victor has a very good family. Now, I'm going to give my blessing for your marriage."

The one piece of advice Dad gave me was: "Don't think of moving back and settling in India again. The society here still is not ready to let you live happily here. Make your life in America after this."

So, even as we were preparing to get married, there was some anxiety back home about the different backgrounds of our families. When we got married here, we actually celebrated these differences and it became quite an exceptional gathering of people in 1975. We had our civil ceremony at the Oak Park City Hall, near where I lived at the time. This little city just north of Detroit still has a large Jewish population. As we arranged to get married, the mayor of Oak Park became quite intrigued with the whole idea. I was from a Hindu family and was getting married to a Muslim in a ceremony performed by this mayor, who was Jewish. The mayor was so fascinated by our story that he presented Dad with a key to the city of Oak Park.

At that time, Victor's parents were not able to come for the marriage. And, soon, Victor and I moved to Canada for a few years to complete our studies and to work in the Toronto area. I had converted to Islam just before we got married, but at that time neither Victor nor I were as involved as we are today in Muslim traditions.

This more casual approach to our religious traditions eventually led to some anxiety when I made my first trip back to India to see my family and to meet Victor's parents. Because of our schedules, Victor couldn't get away for as much time as I planned to spend—a couple of months. This was a very important trip. After living in the Toronto area for about five years, Victor and I were about to immigrate back to America and to settle permanently in the U.S. In January of 1979, our first child, Sami, was born and, by early 1980, we wanted the family back in India to have a chance to see little Sami. As it turned out, Sami celebrated his first birthday in India.

As I set off on this long journey, I had no idea how the meeting with Victor's parents would go. His mother's name was Hasina Sultana, and his family was very well-known in their region of central India. Victor's grandfather was chief justice of the Hyderabad court and his uncles also were justices.

I had not studied much about Islam at that point. I did not cover my hair like I do now. I didn't even know all of the Arabic prayers that are important in Islam. What would Victor's parents think about me? I heard the old jokes about problems with "in-laws" and I began to worry. This new relationship was going to be even more complex in my case.. I was coming from another faith and I knew that Victor's mother was very religious.

My first stop in India was Bombay, where I stayed with my family for a couple of weeks. Then, my parents made the train trip with Sami and me to Hyderabad—a journey of about eight hours. We rode on the old-style trains, in which the compartment doors opened right onto the platform.

As the miles passed, I did get a little bit scared about what would be awaiting us when we arrived. I was wearing loose Indian clothing, which was appropriate, but the type of scarf I was wearing did not completely cover my hair in the Muslim style.

When we finally arrived at the station, we had not even left the train when one of Victor's younger sisters showed up at the door of our compartment. She had come to look me over. But as she reached out to hug me, I could feel the strength and the warmth in that hug. I could feel her love reaching out to me. Then, she said, "You look nice! And, there's nothing to worry about. Mummie will love you. She is looking forward to seeing you."

Still, I wondered what would happen. We stepped out of the train, and everything was so loud on the platform! Many Indians travel by train, and the crowd was rushing in all directions. Porters were shouting. I put Sami into his stroller to make it easier to walk through all the people.

Where was Victor's family in that big crowd? I could not see them at first. And how should I greet them? In Hindu custom, we kneeled down and touched an elder's feet out of respect, but this was not the case in Islam, I knew. In Islam, the only one you kneel to is Allah, and you show affection for other people with an embrace. Would I get this right?

Then, I saw through the crowd these people with flowers—a huge garland of white jasmine and roses. It was my mother-in-law, my father-in-law, another sister-in-law and her husband and kids. They all were waiting to greet me with these flowers, which they placed around my neck. This was such a warm welcome full of embraces.

Our entire time in Hyderabad was wonderful! I knew very little about Muslim prayers and my mother-in-law brought in a teacher each day, so I remember that time, as well, because it's when I learned a great deal about the basics of prayer in Islam. Victor's mother was a petite lady with nice features and a particular way of carrying herself, so that you could tell she came from a noble family. She liked to wear a sari and sometimes wore flowers in her hair.

Later, she came to live with us in our home in America for 12 years, before she passed away in 1994—and she became one of my best friends. It was so easy to love her. She did things like quietly praise me to other people, when I wasn't around. I first heard about this from friends who would tell me what she had said. That surprised me, at first. But it taught me that all those old stereotypes about "in-laws" were totally false—at least in my family. I was blessed to have those years with her.

Here's another example: At first, I wasn't a good cook—at least not in the Hyderabadi style of cooking—but she was such a good teacher. I cannot recall her ever criticizing me. At first, she would cook things herself and show me what she was doing. As she got older, she would sit with me in the kitchen as I cooked. When the food was done, she only ever said good things about the dishes.

She had one specific spot in our family room—her chair, where she would settle in each day and begin her routine. She loved soap operas on television and she also loved to pray with beads, chanting the names of God with the beads. She also would turn on an audio player near her chair to help with the chanting. All three things were going on at the same time: soap operas, the beads and the audio for the chanting. She loved it.

And I loved her. Sometimes I think about that train ride across India as I wondered what she would be like. As I wondered: Would she accept me?

As it turned out, our family was blessed. And, most importantly, so much of what she did in our friendship was quietly done. She always used to say to me: "Whatever good you do for others, never boast of it. If you do, your goodness will be washed away. Whatever good you can do in life for someone else—do it quietly and with the full intention of your heart."

CHAPTER 29

Sofia B. Latif
Balancing Faith and Family

> *Sometimes my father and my mother's uncle would debate some of the teachings— the way that I imagine other families debate politics—but then they would sit down and have dinner together.*

Sofia is a practicing Muslim whose life has been influenced by the differing religious backgrounds of her parents. Her mother is Shahina Begg, who tells her story in the previous chapter. Sofia attributes her commitment to issues of unity and diversity to the example her parents set throughout her childhood.

Throughout my life, my parents taught me to build relationships based upon the values that I share with others. Through their example, I learned to move beyond just tolerance for religious diversity—to actually love and embrace people of all faiths.

My parents met in college in the United States, although they are both Indian immigrants. My mother is from Bombay and was raised Hindu, and my father is from a Muslim family from Hyderabad. When they married, my mother decided to convert to Islam, and when my brothers and I were born, we were raised Muslim.

From a very young age, I remember learning to read the Quran from my father's mother. I attended Sunday School at the mosque, prayed five times a day alongside my parents, and fasted during the month of Ramadan. Islam was a central part of my life, and I was very proud to be Muslim. But unlike many of my Sunday School friends, there was a large part of my life that did not revolve around Islam.

Often during school breaks, my family would travel to visit my mother's relatives. My Hindu cousins sometimes spent entire summers at our home and, during weddings and other big celebrations, both sides of my family would come together. During these times, my parents fostered a welcoming environment where the tensions often associated with differing cultures and traditions could not be felt. Sometimes my father and my mother's uncle would talk and even debate about religious teachings—the way that I imagine other families debate about politics—but then they would sit down and have dinner together. Both my father and mother's uncle are devout followers of their separate faiths, but they did not allow the differences in their religious beliefs to interfere with family relationships.

Reflecting now, I realize how my parents—despite the challenges brought by religious diversity—prioritized the values of hospitality, of respect to elders and of family. My brothers and I were not taught to see the lines that religion often places between people, but rather, we were shown how to love and admire the humanity that unifies them.

When I joined the sixth grade at a public middle school, I decided to begin wearing the traditional Muslim headscarf, knowing that I would be the only one to do so. It was a difficult transition, but even at such a young age, I was firm in my faith and confident that when others began to know me, they would accept me for who I was. My parents' example, in so many subtle and obvious ways, had given me proof that people who ultimately shared the same values would find friendship and amity. My best friends throughout my middle and high school years were Shannon Fink, a Jew, and Alka Tandon, a Hindu.

Today, I recognize that my passion for working toward creating pluralistic societies with religious and cultural understanding is a direct result of my upbringing. During my senior year in high school, when I heard about the "Reuniting the Children of Abraham" project, I was truly excited to get involved. This was an opportunity to work with young adults from over a dozen different racial, cultural, socioeconomic and religious backgrounds to tell a common story—the story of how Abraham's two sons, Isaac and Ishmael, the patriarchs of two great religions, came together upon their father's death to bury him. The goal was to use this story as an example for how our communities today can overcome the hate and fear that divides us. As I worked with this diverse group on developing the storyline for the play, I once again found myself searching for the values that connected us and brought us together. It was only after we, as a group, were able to overcome the tensions of diversity, that we could co-create what has now become an award-winning

production and documentary that has traveled across the
U.S., Jerusalem and Jordan.

Colophon

This book was produced using methods that separate content from presentation. Doing so increases the flexibility and accessibility of the content and allows us to generate editions in different presentation formats quickly and easily.

The content is stored in a standard XML format called DocBook version 5.0 (www.docbook.org.) Adobe InDesign®, the Oxygen® XML Editor and Microsoft Word® were used in the production.

- The print edition is set in Minion Pro and Myriad Pro type.
- Editing by David Crumm.
- Copy editing and styling by Stephanie Fenton.
- Digital encoding and print layout by John Hile.
- Cover art and design by Rick Nease (www.RickNease.com.)

Notes:

If you liked this book, you may also like:

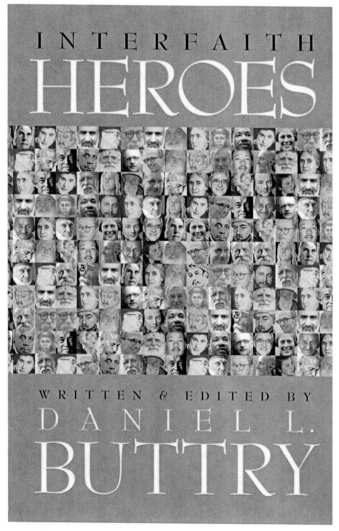

INTERFAITH HEROES

WRITTEN & EDITED BY DANIEL L. BUTTRY

A Daily Reader of Inspirational Stories about Leaders Reaching Out to Spiritually Unite People and Build Stronger Communities.

http://www.ReadTheSpirit.com/Interfaith_Heroes/

ISBN: 978-1-934879-00-9

If you liked this book, you may also like:

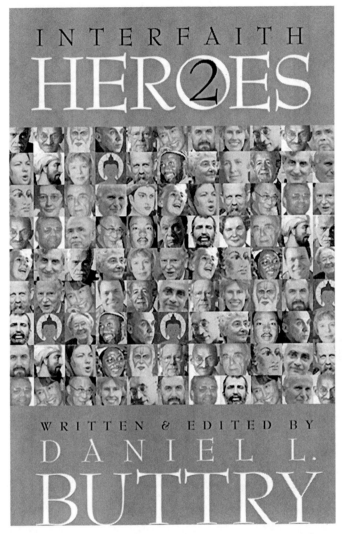

If you liked this book, you may also like:

"Rodney Curtis can find wonder in a 3/8-inch socket wrench and laughter in just about anything. He's a treasure and so is his book"
—*Detroit News* Columnist Neal Rubin

http://www.ReadTheSpirit.com/Spiritual_Wanderer/

ISBN: 978-1-934879-07-8